The Talking Draft Method

Hollywood's Secret to a Fast First Draft

FREDERICK GOOLTZ

THE TALKING DRAFT METHOD

HOLLYWOOD'S SECRET FOR A FAST FIRST DRAFT

ISBN: 9798224573875

Talking Draft Media
Los Angeles

www.TalkingDraft.com

DEDICATION

This book is dedicated to Maggie Moon. Not a single thing would be possible if not for you.

"If you are using dialogue — say it aloud as you write it. Only then will it have the sound of speech."

- John Steinbeck

CONTENTS

"When I'm writing the first draft, I'm constantly reminding myself that I'm simply shoveling sand into a box so that later I can build castles."

- Jordan Peele

INTRODUCTION

to

USE THE TALKING DRAFT METHOD FOR A FAST FIRST DRAFT

The Talking Draft Method is the fastest way for playwrights or screenwriters to create scenes. The steps are simple:

1. A writer records audio of themselves improvising all the dialogue and the action lines,

2. The audio is transcribed,

3. The text is reformatted into a script.

This is not new, it is actually one of old Hollywood's best-kept secrets. Some of the most prolific writers have used the Talking Draft Method to quickly produce first drafts and dialogue-heavy scenes. But few can afford the full-time stenographers these A-list writers have while they record themselves acting out a scene. Until now.

Screenwriters and technologists have finally customized tools to easily create fast first drafts for the screen using the Talking Draft Method.

This book will explain the history and science behind the Talking Draft Method, and it will provide a helpful guide for screenwriters setting out to write their first drafts.

Your finished first draft is the goal of this book. All of the techniques and tricks described in this book are engineered to get you creating your first drafts fast. The website application that accompanies this book at www.TalkingDraft.com is also engineered for your fast first drafts.

But finishing your first draft is not the end of your journey – it is only the beginning of the dozens of rewrites that every script always needs. Subsequently, this book will also help you on that larger quest; by the end of the book you will be armed with some of the best outlining and revision approaches currently in use by industry pros.

The easiest way to get good is to become prolific. It takes practice. The Talking Draft Method is the absolute easiest way to achieve prolificacy. So learn The Talking Draft Method, crank out your stories, and become great. You have it in you – let's hear it.

WHEN

WHEN HOWARD HAWKS INVENTED THE METHOD

The Talking Draft Method dates to the Golden Age of Hollywood.

The story goes that in 1934, novelist William Faulkner's Hollywood career was circling the drain. His friend, film director Howard Hawks came to the rescue.

Howard Hawks knew there was an executive at MGM hungry to get Hawks under contract, so on a Friday, Hawks whetted the executive's appetite saying that Hawks had decided what he wanted his next two projects to be, and that he would deliver the screenplays "next week."

Hawks quickly optioned the rights to two of Faulkner's short stories. So Hawks temporarily had the permission to develop the stories into film scripts, and if he successfully sold the projects to a studio, then Faulkner would get a big payday.

Hawks then borrowed a massive reel-to-reel audio tape recorder the size of a refrigerator called a "Marconi Machine" from the BBC and brought the hulking pile of technology to an empty office at MGM.

On Saturday morning, Hawks and Faulkner sat down and wrote two screenplays in one weekend. How exactly Hawks achieved this feat begins to give shape to understanding the Method.

Firstly, whenever a storyteller is "free" to speak as freely as they wish, then tight, prescribed <u>outlining</u> becomes even more paramount to the task. Some raconteurs ramble, Hawks surely knew this about his friend.

Howard Hawks came into the empty office armed with Faulkner's stories already annotated. Notably, the short stories did not have much dialogue. Hawks had underlined the most vital bits of narrative action in Faulkner's prose and marked places where dialogue needed to be added.

Hawks' markups of Faulkner's stories included arrows and numerals to reorder sections of the prose, keeping the stories inside tight Hollywood structures. Hawks turned on the audio recording machine.

Using these markups as his outline, Hawks began reading the opening "Action" sentences of the first scene into the microphone. Faulkner simply watched as Hawks set up the scene.

As the voice recorder rolled tape, the director came to the first point in the story where a scene needed new dialogue. Hawks simply tilted the microphone towards Faulkner and encouraged him with a nod. Faulkner then improvised new dialogue to flesh out the moment. Hawks interjected occasionally to add action lines.

Scene-by-scene, the two fleshed out Faulkner's concise short stories hewing to Hawks' notes. When Faulkner was creating the new dialogue, he spoke as all the characters in each scene - as if performing the conversation by himself, eyes closed. No "he said, she said."

Soon, Faulkner was doing both — dictating new action lines and acting-out new dialogue, even donning the voices of the different characters in his mind's eye.

Once Faulkner was up to speed, Hawks' task turned to merely keeping Faulkner to his Hollywood outline. The two friends acted and worked their way through both stories in that little room. They wrapped the weekend with two finished feature scripts on the reels of audio tape. The first drafts, at least.

That is the second most important aspect of the Talking Draft Method after outlining: <u>momentum</u>. Forward momentum is the power behind the first draft. One must move forward, only forward, until the story is done.

Legend has it that on Monday, a stenographer typed up all the audio tapes. Then those pages were reformatted by MGM's script assistants. Satisfied with the drafts, Hawks' producers at the studio cut a check to Faulkner, thus keeping him afloat.

The projects fell through, as nearly all do, but that didn't matter. Hawks' intervention was a success. William Faulkner was on his feet - from 1934 to 1954 Faulkner went on to work on around 50 films.

Over the decades since Howard Hawks, many writers in Hollywood have used some version of this trick to crank out a fast first draft. For a while, the Talking Draft Method was even named after Howard Hawks.

But Howard Hawks did not invent storytellers using dictation, nor did he even invent using technology to assist in the act of dictating a narrative. No, Hawks may have introduced this method of writing to the art form of film, but the history of speech-to-text is older than the Bible.

The history of storytellers dictating their tales is ancient and storied…

WHO

The Honor Roll of Story Dictation

If you believe the legend, Greek poet Homer probably dictated the entire *Iliad* and *Odyssey* because, according to tradition, he was blind.

Throughout the centuries since, some of the greatest storytellers in the world created many of their classics by talking. It's no surprise that so many of those who became proficient at dictation also became hugely prolific. This is because not only does the Talking Draft Method help you finish your first draft faster than any other method, but because the first draft usually takes the longest time to write with traditional methods, it stands to reason that those who talk their first drafts end up getting far more work done over the course of their careers because they are not hung-up as often by the "first draft trap."

Sometimes, it may be a physical impairment that causes a writer to try speech-to-text dictation. For example, after he lost his eyesight in the 1650s, John Milton dictated the entirety of *Paradise Lost* to his daughter who worked as his amanuensis – a specific kind of literary assistant who takes dictation.

Other times, it is ambition and a fertile imagination that brings a writer into the Talking Draft camp. French playwright Voltaire was an extraordinarily prolific maestro. Voltaire wrote more than 50 plays, dozens of treatises on science, politics and philosophy, and several books on history. He kept up his prodigious output by spending up to 18 hours a day dictating to secretaries, often while still in bed. Ninety-percent of his output was in the handwriting of his assistant Jean-Louis Wagnière.

Two-hundred years ago Stendhal, the innovative French writer, dictated his renowned novel *The Charterhouse of Parma* to a secretary in under two months.

Nineteenth century master storyteller Alexandre Dumas, author of *The Three Musketeers, The Count of Monte Cristo* (and 158 other books) also dictated his novels to a secretary before they were fashioned into his acclaimed works. He actually started a production studio where he hired multiple writers to continue projects that he started, often by dictation, checking in with each project to make edits and adjustments.

Over 120 years ago, Fyodor Dostoyevsky dictated many of his novels to a stenographer - Anna Grigorievna - with whom he fell in love and later married. Dostoyevsky first used Talking Draft Method to get out of financial trouble. The great Russian novelist was under contract to produce a book with a horrible deadline but he had gambled away his publisher's advance. If he failed to deliver, he was contractually bound to pay off the advance with manual labor. His friends and family convinced him to put out a classified advertisement in a newspaper for a stenographer to take his dictation. The first book which he mentally composed and dictated aloud was his novel *The Gambler*. This became his normal working method.

After suffering with arthritis in his mid-fifties, Victorian-era writer Henry James hired a secretary to transcribe his spoken words, ushering in a new era of productivity for him which culminated in *The Wings of the Dove*, now widely regarded as one of his finest works.

Audio recording machines were invented in the late 19th century, and were immediately incorporated into the workflow of many prolific writers. American master Mark Twain was the first. After writing the start of his *Autobiography* with a typewriter, he felt that the work lacked the spontaneity and free-wheeling voice of his popular lectures, which were akin to a stand-up comedian's monologue. Twain began dictating his *Autobiography* onto one of Thomas Edison's phonograph recording machines, then having the wax cylinder played back for an assistant who transcribed the audio.

It's largely forgotten that English Prime Minister Winston Churchill was massively published in his day – after all, he won the Nobel Prize for Literature. Not only was Churchill's four volume epic *A History of the English-Speaking People* entirely dictated, but almost all of his newspaper and magazine articles were dictated too. His memorandums in parliament were all dictated, his private letters were dictated; all in all, he dictated millions of words throughout his career.

In the middle of the 20th century, audio recording devices finally got small enough for mass market users. For decades, portable "Dictaphone" machines were used by politicians, business executives, doctors, lawyers, writers, and others to record correspondence, notes, and drafts of stories. The writer or their assistants would then listen to the recording and type up the tapes for review. Often, documents would be reformatted and revised again. Even with all those post-recording steps, the Dictaphone speech-to-text process was fast. And for creative writers it was especially useful. Many writers used Dictaphones...

Erle Stanley Gardner, the author of the *Perry Mason* novel series was a two-finger typist but thanks to his Dictaphone tape recorder, his output was overwhelming. Literally 141 of his books were in print at the time of his death. His books have sold more than 320 million copies in 37 languages. Gardner's work habits were legendary: Rising before dawn, he would begin the day by dictating new novels for several hours. He employed a pool of typists to transcribe the recordings and he would spend the afternoons revising and preparing his manuscripts to send to the publisher. This productivity landed Gardner in the Guinness Book of Records as the world's fastest novelist. He could dictate up to ten thousand words a day.

Dame Agatha Christie dictated perhaps half of her 66 famous mystery novels. She spent the majority of time with each story creating an outline in her notebook, working out all the plot details before she actually started writing. When the writing started, as her grandson Mathew Prichard explained, "she then used to dictate her stories into a machine called a Dictaphone and then a secretary typed this up into a typescript, which my grandmother would correct by hand."

What Agatha Christie was to mystery novels, Barbara Cartland was to romance novels. She published over 700 books (the most of any author). To get herself in the headspace for storytelling in her particular style, she famously used to lie on a fabulous pink couch with a pink wrap over her shoulders holding one of her many Pekingese dogs in her arms. Eyes closed, she would then dictate her saucy romance tales. She would have several transcribing secretaries around her taking down different stories so she could talk through more than one novel at the same time.

Frank Yerby, a famous American historical novelist, began using a tape-based dictation system for some of his novels while living in Europe. His thirty-five historical novels ranged from the Athens of Pericles and Biblical times, to Europe in the Dark Ages, to the Antebellum South.

Richard Powers wrote his National Book Award-winning novel *The Echo Maker* using dictation software. During an interview with *Wired* magazine, he endorsed writing via dictation by pointing out that, "Typing is a highly unnatural activity, and your writing style ends up reflecting the cognitive shackles. When I started to use the [voice recorder], things that are extremely difficult to do on a word processor opened up to me."

There was a time when Isaac Asimov developed problems with his eyesight so he bought a dictation machine. He dictated his stories and then his wife Gertrude transcribed his tapes on the typewriter. He wrote several stories this way. The two only stopped this working arrangement when his wife gave birth to their first child.

In the 1960s, Aldous Huxley suffered from failing eyesight and so he dictated some of his last works to his wife Laura.

Contemporary science fiction writer Kevin J. Anderson records himself talking out his first drafts. He is the author of 56 bestsellers, with more than 23 million books in print worldwide. Also, Dan Brown, author of *The Da Vinci Code*, recently revealed that he dictates all his rough drafts using speech-to-text software.

Dictation in Hollywood

After Howard Hawks brought storytelling dictation into the screenwriting realm, the practice caught on very quickly. For the last 90 years, many writers in Hollywood have used some version of this trick to crank out a fast first draft of their screenplays.

In addition to Howard Hawks, many directors who also write have had a similar knack for seeing the whole story in their mind's eye. When using the Talking Draft Method, the job of a writer-director such as Alfred Hitchcock simply becomes one of describing what they see. Screenwriter Stirling Silliphant learned this firsthand when he was hired on Hitchcock's anthology TV series *Alfred Hitchcock Presents*.

Silliphant once described how he was ushered into Hitchcock's office and sat down before a typewriter. "Hitchcock dictated the script to me — shot by shot, including camera movements and opticals. He actually had already SEEN the finished film." Silliphant gladly took the dictation and the screenplay credit. In total, Silliphant was credited with writing 11 episodes for Hitchcock. Some of which he actually wrote.

Winning Academy Awards for his comedies and dramas, Billy Wilder was one of the most brilliant and versatile writer-directors of Hollywood's golden age. Working on 60 films over 50 years, an incredible twelve of Billy Wilder's scripts were nominated for Academy Awards including *The Apartment* and *Sunset Boulevard*. In 1959, Wilder partnered with writer-producer I.A.L. "Iz" Diamond, a collaboration that remained until the end of both men's careers. Billy Wilder and Iz Diamond used to tape-record their jokey banter around the office — some of which made its way into their witty masterpieces.

For decades, writers for stage and screen often used the Talking Draft Method to capture the rhythms of stylized speech when doing a dialogue pass. Playwrights Harold Pinter and Arthur Miller did just this for the Broadway and West End stages.

Playwright and screenwriter Sidney Sheldon was prominent from the 1930s to the 1970s. First working on Broadway, Sheldon began writing musicals for the stage while continuing to write screenplays for both

MGM Studios and Paramount Pictures. He earned a reputation as a prolific writer; for example, at one time, he had three musicals on Broadway, while one of his five Broadway plays won a Tony Award, and one of his screenplays won the Academy Award.

During his 20 years in television, Sheldon created many hit TV shows, sometimes with more than one show on the air at once. Sheldon wrote almost every single episode of all his shows. For example, on *I Dream of Jeannie*, Sheldon wrote 115 of the show's 139 episodes.

Like other prolific writers who used the Talking Draft Method, Sheldon's writing routine was simple, as he explained:

"Each morning from 9 until noon, I had a secretary at the studio take all calls. I mean every single call. I wrote each morning — or rather, dictated — and then I faced the TV business."

On the best days, Sheldon dictated 50 pages. In addition to his scripts, he wrote all of his 18 novels by dictating the first drafts. His 18 novels have sold over 300 million copies in 51 languages. Sheldon is consistently cited as one of the top-10 best-selling fiction writers of all time.

In the mid 1940s, Paramount hired legendary detective writer and screenwriter Raymond Chandler to write a rush script based on his unfinished novel, *The Blue Dahlia*. Due to the short timeframe, the studio began shooting with a partial script, but quickly the filming caught up to the script. The producer of the film met with Chandler to find out how he could finish the script as quickly as possible. Chandler presented a list of his requirements:

(1) Two cars with drivers available 24×7 to deliver script pages to the studio, get a doctor who could fill him with vitamins, and a maid who could buy him alcohol;

(2) Secretaries to take dictation;

(3) A direct line to the producer.

Chandler knew he wrote best in his flow state when inebriated. The producer agreed to the terms, and over the next eight days, Chandler cranked out the rest of the script.

In the early 1970s screenwriter Ernest Tidyman was an A-List hitmaker known for his Oscar-winning script *The French Connection*. He worked best when driving cross-country from LA to Connecticut dictating his screenplays onto tape which he'd then have transcribed. This is how (and where) he wrote *High Plains Drifter* for Clint Eastwood.

Rod Serling – Master of the Talking Draft Method

Rod Serling was an award-winning screenwriter, playwright and TV producer who massively shaped the early years of TV. He penned scripts for most of the anthology TV shows at the time including, *Kraft Theatre, Studio One, The U.S. Steel Hour, Playhouse 90*, and 12 feature films.

Most famously, Serling wrote 92 *Twilight Zone* episodes and 36 scripts for his TV series *Night Gallery*. This staggering output was aided by his dedicated use of The Talking Draft Method.

In the '50s and '60s Rod Serling was never far from his beloved Dictaphone machine. Serling recorded his scenes onto 1,152 "dictabelts" which are now finally getting the digital conversion they need.

According to the Rod Serling Memorial Foundation, the writer began dictating scripts early in his television career to save time. The Foundation, which has been administered by his family since his death at age 50, suggests that his use of The Talking Draft Method greatly "influenced his writing and his mastery of dialogue."

Researchers at the Wisconsin Center for Film and Theatre Research, where Serling's tapes are being digitized, have listened to his dictabelts to find that the writer not only dictated the dialogue without uttering character names (e.g. "How are you? / Really bad. / Can I help?") but Serling also seamlessly included action lines containing his scene descriptions. This approach remains the core of the Talking Draft Method today.

Rod Serling's use of the Talking Draft Method made his prolific output legendary in his own time. He created hundreds of scripts on thousands of Dictaphone reels. Serling was able to remain in a creative flow state for the runtime of his stories, and in one sitting he could produce a first draft. This is surely a huge factor in his enviable accomplishment of 100-plus produced scripts before age 50.

New Dictation Technology

When screenwriter Aaron Sorkin started his habit of driving around town with an audio recorder as he barreled through his dialogue, the whole Talking Draft Method process was still manual, as it had been since the days of Howard Hawks. Sorkin used script assistants to type up his recorded dialogue.

"When I'm writing, I'm playing all the parts; I'm saying the lines out loud…it's the greatest feeling."

- Aaron Sorkin

David Milch dictated all his *NYPD Blue* scripts himself while laying on the floor of his office. His typist at a desk would take his dictation. On *Deadwood*, Milch would write scenes and shoot them in one day.

David Lynch outlines on index cards using the Eight Sequence structure [See pg 75], then he dictates dialogue and action to an assistant.

For decades, every unsung amanuensis in Hollywood tending to the transcription needs of some of the most prolific screenwriters has had to cope with the same big problem: More than the effort of actual transcription, it is the issue of figuring out "who-says-what-when" in dialogue which has always been the thorniest problem facing the amanuensis-style script assistants. This task, marking who-says-what-when is known by linguists and technologists as "diarization."

Modern speech-to-text AI features algorithmic diarization, meaning it can automatically figure out who is saying what even during a chaotic conversation between multiple people. But this amazing technology does nothing for the screenwriter because every "person" in our conversations is actually voiced by us – and our one voice. Because writers write alone, today's automatic speech-to-text software does not solve our problem of diarization.

All speech-to-text gives us is a long block of transcribed text, requiring us to go through the words and manually break it up into many chunks of dialog and action. From the reading of words alone it is very easy to mistake *who* was supposed to say *what*. To mitigate this weak spot, script assistants also needed to listen to the audio tapes while reading the transcription output in order to double-check any unclear diarization changes of dialog speaker.

However, not every writer is also a great actor like Harold Pinter was, so the script assistant listening back to the audio tapes sometimes still struggled to figure out "who says what when," and could not tell when the "Action lines" began or ended. If the writer was not acting broadly enough, a common outcome was guessing wrong and mixing up the scene.

For people who wanted to cut down on diarization errors, there were no good solutions. No writer wants to utter clunky voice commands like "action line" or "character name Jim" before each line of dialogue in order to format aloud. Storytellers don't want anything that bucks us out of our creative flow-state or knocks us off the story's pace. Constantly having to say the name of the character is just as annoying (and needlessly time-consuming) as having to say "tab-tab." Some systems annoyingly even require writers to say the name of each punctuation mark aloud.

Thankfully, technology has become better since the early 2000s. Today's speech-to-text AI now comes with 95% accuracy, and very intelligent automatic grammar and spell-check.

Nevertheless, since the invention of speech-to-text technology, it has been clear that screenwriters and playwrights needed some sort of manual diarization. We needed to be able to note, with our hands, *who says what when* <u>as</u> we improvised our scenes.

Many solutions to this problem have been tried over the decades. In each, the writer records themselves "acting-out" the scene's dialogue and narrating the action lines, meanwhile her hands manipulate different machines. Some writers tried to use stenography hardware but found that the learning curve was too steep and required too much focus on the hands instead of the storytelling.

Other screenwriters recorded themselves to tape for speech-to-text processing while their hands pressed speaker label buttons on a custom timestamping device. But all of these require the writer to go through the tape again watching the timestamps while looking at the speech-to-text output in order to actually format the script. This was such a slow and laborious process that when the custom timestamping software did not survive the retirement of Windows 95, it was for the better.

The lowest budget version that ever approximated manual diarization required the writer to act-out the scene while one hand pressed a button on a lap stopwatch, and while the other hand pressed numbers on a keyboard which corresponded to who-says-what. The keyboard entered the numbers (character names) into a spreadsheet. Then it took many table merges to combine the list of lap times with the speech-to-text beside the correct dialogue speaker. Manipulating all the documents with requisite find-replace functions took an exceedingly long time and was extremely complicated. Additionally, during storytelling itself, coordination between left hand and right hand was very difficult.

Now that technologists have a better understanding of what screenwriters have been doing to hack solutions to the problem of manual diarization, there is finally specialized software dedicated to the Talking Draft Method. No writer needs to hire a personal assistant or amanuensis to do the Talking Draft Method ever again.

Recently, the webapp www.TalkingDraft.com achieved flawless manual diarization by combining the best ideas from previous solutions to create the only way to write a perfect Talking Draft on the fly. Today, thanks to this new technology, one of classic Hollywood's best-kept secrets can be anyone's secret weapon for a fast first draft.

What had taken Howard Hawks' script assistants over 100 combined hours to accomplish in a week (transcribing the text, achieving proper dialogue diarization, changing some of the dictated text into Action lines, adding Scene Location "slug" lines, and adding character names before their correct lines of dialogue) now happens instantly. www.TalkingDraft.com has eliminated all of those post-recording steps which have long bothered Hollywood transcription script assistants.

With www.TalkingDraft.com, rather than have your transcribed text get painstakingly reformatted by hand later, you format it _and_ manually diarize the dialog as you improvise your scene. This innovation fully automates the time-tested and time-saving screenwriting method that was proudly used by some of the greatest writers to ever work the craft.

The webapp at www.TalkingDraft.com also offers automated beat sheet generation with a free beat sheet calculator to create the kind of step-outlines that truly power a Talking Draft. Your outline keeps your talking on track. One needs to simply fill up their outline with scene reminders, location slug lines, and character names. You dictate your dialogue and action lines.

The Talking Draft Method has been the fastest way to produce the first draft of a screenplay since its invention in 1936. This method is an inspired use of technology to capture the power of the creative flow state which is the key to generating a mountainous legacy of classic hits. Now, this method is available to anyone.

Everyone, especially aspiring writers, would be wise to utilize The Talking Draft Method. The following chapters will explain why it is so important, effective, and how exactly to use it.

WHY

Storytelling and Voice

Dictation can literally capture your voice.

Writing coaches always talk about capturing "your voice," which is a hard to define goal that every writer chases so as to be read as original or authentic.

If you're speaking aloud and just letting your story flow naturally… that *is* your voice. If you're transcribing the audio into a rough draft via speech-to-text dictation software, then you will absolutely find your voice. After all, it is you speaking.

You cannot fail to find your own voice if you listen to yourself tell your own story as it unfolds in your head, retaining elements of your speech patterns and thought processes upon re-drafting.

The real Samuel L. Clemens was well-read, highly-educated, cosmopolitan and lived in erudite elite Hartford, Connecticut. "Mark Twain" was his literary persona. His most beloved writing voice was literally Clemens' impersonation of a Missouri country bumpkin.

Late in life, when he was writing his *Autobiography*, Twain wanted to return to his country bumpkin voice which had made him famous, but it had been years since his lecture circuit tours where he performed as Twain and he'd written several novels in a different style – Clemens was out of practice playing "The Innocent."

Around this time he heard about Thomas Edison's invention of an audio-recording phonograph machine. Procuring one of the first consumer recording machines, Twain talked his *Autobiography* out loud because he knew that performing and remaining in that "Innocent" character's headspace would be key to recapturing the conversational tone and style he needed to be "Twain" again.

Good writing often sounds like natural speech. Some writers today are able to sound exactly like Jane Austen in an English sitting room and have it sound natural. However, most writers' voices today sound very much more like themselves, in modern times, in their modern minds. Though speaking may be nearly effortless, typing dialogue is often the opposite – this is true whether or not you are writing a historical voice.

Writing coaches sometimes advise us to "write like you speak." But that's like telling someone to "dance like you walk." Sure, walking comes naturally to some people, but that still has no bearing on how difficult it is for most of us to dance. There is so much about the act of writing that makes it hard to have our output feel as effortless as speaking.

It is immeasurably easier to adopt a consistent voice from talking aloud than it is to maintain a strong voice via typing. Simply too much can go wrong with a keyboard. Every moment we second-guess our word choice, or any moment when we re-consider our punctuation, or double-check our spelling, anytime we mistype anything, any grammar snafu can derail us from the natural flow of the story as it wants to be heard.

Every derailment breaks the flow. The easiest way to maintain a consistent voice across a long piece of storytelling is to get your headspace into the tone, style and attitude that is right for your work, and then talk *as that voice* while an audio recorder rolls - preferably an audio capture device with quality automatic speech-to-text enabled.

Mark Twain knew this was true in 1888. We know it to be true today.

WHAT IS A WRITER'S VOICE

A unique voice is a seamless combination of the writer's point-of-view, her style, tone, syntax, and her themes.

A writer's point-of-view is your perspective on the world, how you judge it, and how your background influences the types of stories you choose to tell and what your characters do and say about the world that you've presented for us to also judge.

Conviction is the foundation of voice. Many novice writers don't approach their stories with the sort of strong opinions that result in strong voices. To convey a voice, a writer has to have specific positions about the ideas present in the story, and strong emotions about the themes expressed through the fate of her characters. She needs to put those positions on the page.

A writer has to know what she wants to say, and figure out how to say it, but also, and especially, reveal herself within the telling. This art is like casting the writer's shadow across the work – except this shadow *enlightens* those elements that resonate closest with her opinion about the story. It is this enlightening by a writer's light touches that will make any story more vivid. The more enthusiastic a writer is about adding her lightening to the plot in order to highlight certain themes, the stronger the voice will be in that piece of writing.

Think of voice in terms of music: There are certain singers who have a particular "sound." When a singer has a distinct sound, you know exactly who they are from his first note or phrase. Both Sam Cooke and Nat King Cole always sound like they're smiling while singing - but Cole's texture is smokier, a light gravel from too many cigarettes vibrates atop the dimpled cheeks that you can hear in his singing.

It is the same for writers. If you have a distinct or unique writing voice, it will be present on page one, and it should remain strong throughout the first ten pages. The writer's voice sets up what type of journey we will go on and the style or tone in which we will travel. What critics call "voice" can arise in brief, subtle moments while being present consistently throughout the work.

When we speak of tone in screenwriting, we're often talking about attitude. Does the writer like the world of the story, dislike her antihero? Does the writer want us to hate the villain for his politics? All these tiny markers that a writer sprinkles judiciously throughout the piece serve to inform the reader of what kind of film this will end up being. If it is a tongue-in-cheek mockumentary, then the writing needs tongue-in-cheek asides that capture her tone and actively communicate the meta style.

It's not enough to just say on the title page "a drama" and then paint the plot by numbers. The writing itself needs to jerk tears out of even the coldest-hearted reader with very few words.

The style in which you write includes tone, but elements of style are also as specific as word choice. Think of what quirky or stylized word choice and syntax will do for your style.

In screenwriting, even the sentence structure of our descriptions and action lines convey style. Good action lines often sound poetic, and dialogue is often optimized for efficiency and clarity.

The style of dialogue communicates everything from the time period to a presentational acting style. For example, if you're inventing goofy words, you will surely communicate a tone that suggests a certain style of comedy.

Above and beyond dialogue, a writer with a unique voice usually has common themes that show up in many different pieces of work, regardless of genre. Strong themes arise when the writer's point-of-view is pointed and powerfully felt. If you don't have unique or insightful things to say about the human condition then maybe writing is not for you.

In the same way one could describe the differences between Beyoncé and Taylor Swift, writers with strong voices leave similar traces on readers. Shonda Rhimes has a vibrant, provocative voice that uses flowing monologues and rapid-fire dialogue. Phoebe Waller-Bridge efficiently paints fraught and deep relationships while juxtaposing moments of softness with punches of elegant crassness.

You need to create enough screenplays, experimenting with different mixes of your perspective stampings, your emotional enlightening, and your style markings until a singular voice emerges.

The ultimate goal is to get to the point where any reader of your script, regardless of its genre or format, should know it's your work. These individualizing elements also communicate that the writer is in firm control of the story. This reassurance is appreciated by all readers.

WHY IS A WRITER'S VOICE SO IMPORTANT?

Every story has been told. What makes a story unique is the storyteller.

Voice is essential to hook your reader and keep them engaged. Voice also is the difference maker in whether writers get representation and get hired because voice is your whole brand as a writer.

A strong voice makes your script feel more individualistic, it helps it cut through the noise of the reader's script pile. They have hundreds of scripts to read and they want to find one with a strong voice.

A strong voice wakes up the reader. A strong voice shows that you are a dynamic storyteller with power.

A strong voice gives the reader confidence that you are in command of the story, that the reader does not have to work very hard to understand what kind of story this is because you communicate that you are strong enough to sustain this unique mood throughout the whole read – and subsequently, the finished movie will also feel consistent and thoroughly lived-in.

A strong voice makes it feel like nobody else sees the world quite like you. Readers want to discover writers with this power. Good storytelling isn't just entertainment, it's a gift that readers of scripts hope to discover.

Storytelling Not Storywriting

A film script is truly unlike any other piece of writing.

One of the many things that a screenplay needs to do is serve as a blueprint for a film production, and so the structure of the screenplay document itself has been designed so that one page equals one minute of screen time.

This running clock in the mind of the reader puts screenwriting more in the oral tradition of storytelling (instead of in the book publishing tradition). The reader is hearing you tell them the story in real-time. What does this mean for you?

This difference means that pacing is vital — literally how long it takes you to describe things is how long they appear on screen. Another thing this means is that your attitude and point-of-view — the personality that comes through in your action lines — helps sell what kind of movie this is going to be.

All of the qualities that make a story told aloud compelling are the same qualities that make a screenplay reading session entertaining for the reader. Your screenplay document needs to entertain the reader. Obviously dialogue is meant to be heard aloud, but the storyteller's voice in the action lines also must convey enough personality that it communicates genre and tone.

The one writing method that best accentuates precisely those elements is The Talking Draft Method.

Unlearning the Writing Part

It takes time and practice to get used to this style of storytelling versus story-writing. For people who have only ever written papers in school for teachers to ponder, or written stories in the publishing tradition, a screenplay can be hard.

One must first unlearn the habits that come with print writing methods. Foremost amongst those typing elements has to do with pace. The momentum of your story in a screenplay matches the momentum of your storytelling. It should flow.

The problem with composing a screenplay with a keyboard is that it allows you to pause. A keyboard allows you to press "backspace," and to highlight whole sections and "delete" them, as you tinker and edit and tweak. All of that is bad. Do not do that on your first drafts.

Get the story out of you head as a cohesive story. Use your voice to capture your writing voice. Use your energy to capture the dynamics of dialogue, speaking the lines aloud. The Talking Draft Method forces you to get through your story without editing and wasting time. The Talking Draft Method helps you capture your personality as you dictate the tale. The Talking Draft Method puts you more in the oral tradition of storytelling instead of the stultifying world of publishing.

A Strong Sense of Voice

The question of getting a staff writing job on a television show may be too advanced for a book such as this. However, it should be noted that if a career in TV writing is your goal, you need to have extra skills with regard to voice.

A feature writer can succeed with one strong unique voice. But a journeyman staff writer needs to hone the ability to mimic other voices. A TV writer should be able to watch an episode of TV, and/or read a sample episode script of that show, and then mimic the voice.

To do this requires a strong "sense" of voice. This skill comes down to finding ways to replicate the feeling of the original writer's tone. Writers who can match tone, match style, and especially match voice, will get a lot of work if their agents know how to market them.

Think of this as the ability to do impressions of celebrities, which is slightly different than doing a full impersonation of a celebrity.

When a comedian does an impression of a celebrity, they often hook into just a few quirks, one or two characteristic sayings, maybe a peculiar gesture that the celebrity does often. One need not look and sound exactly like the original, but there should be enough of these strong connections to the original's essence that the audience will understand immediately.

However, and this is the really hard part, a writer's unique fingerprint should also show up in their TV staffing work. Your indelible voice is why the showrunner hired you in the first place. They want your individual note added to the chord of their season. This raises the question: How can we have a unique voice that still matches the tone of a show we write on?

This feat is a giant and challenging balancing act. The script that gets you the TV staffing job may be a deeply personal and unique script. Based on its brilliance, your boss will assume that you are able to mimic the show's style. You will still need to practice this skill. To practice, write script samples that ape many different styles of TV shows. In judiciously chosen moments allow your indelible voice to come through without overpowering any part of them.

For more detailed insights, find *The TV Writer's Workbook* by Ellen Sandler. Either way you slice it, you will need to create a lot of scripts to hone your *voice* and also to develop your *sense* of voice.

It stands to reason that the best way to write many scripts is not to get stuck on the first draft of the first one. The best way to write a fast first draft is by using The Talking Draft Method. That's why we're here.

"You can always edit a bad page. You can't edit a blank page."

- Phoebe Waller-Bridge

HOW

How to Avoid the First Draft Trap

According to a 2011 Independent Book Publishers Association (IBPA) survey, 200,000,000 (81%) of Americans feel they have a story in them they should write. Why don't they?

People don't finish because of the same excuse since before Gutenberg invented the printing press: A blank page is scary.

Despite the fear of a blank page, many brave souls still do try to write their story. Every year, during National Novel Writing Month, around a half million aspiring writers take part in The NaNoWriMo challenge, but only 10 to 15% actually finish.

"A bad script WRITTEN is still better than an amazing one THAT ISN'T."

- Taika Waititi

This is the sad fact: Most first drafts don't get finished. But with the Talking Draft Method, a writer never has to face a blank page again. The Method has been engineered to defuse the most common first draft traps:

The two biggest reasons writers give up finishing their first drafts are well known:

1) people try to edit while they write.

2) people skimp on the outline.

Firstly, a great way to keep momentum and not edit while you write is to remember the iron rule…

The Iron Rule

As in ironing clothes.

When we iron a shirt, we tend to return our steaming iron to one portion and then expand that well-ironed bit further. Over and over, returning to the beginning. If we are lucky enough to not *run out of steam* before finishing the job, the result of this ironing style is that one area in your work will be perfect but other parts have been barely touched.

When this principle is applied to storytelling, it looks like the infamous underdrawn horse.

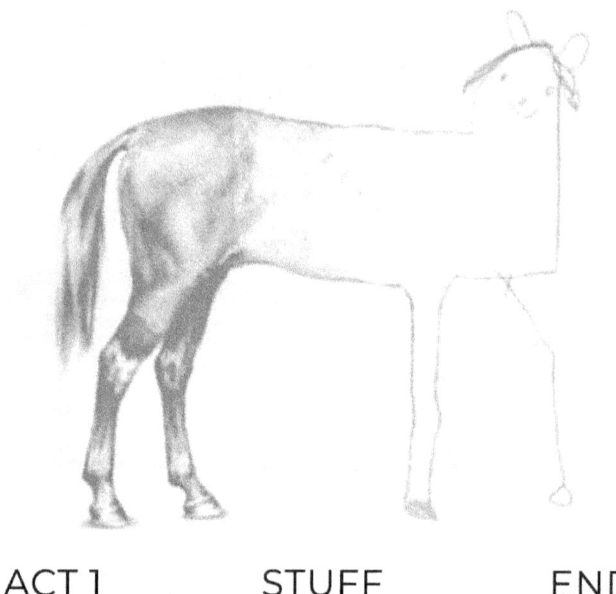

As you can see in the illustration, the first part of the story has been well shaped, all of the extra passes really helped add depth and detail. Then in the middle section, with fewer editing passes and less time refining details, we have basic "stuff." The quality drops off dramatically as we peter out leaving behind a mere sketch.

"Editing as you" go often leads to an uneven script, sometimes with the severity of the underdrawn horse. This urge to edit as we go is one of the classic traps of the first draft. We have to fight this urge.

The Talking Draft Method saves you from this infamous first draft trap by removing text from your sight altogether.

The reasons are simple: Any misspelling will only make you want to stop and press backspace to fix it. Any time you do finish a long and mellifluous sentence, you'll feel the urge to read it back to feel good.

Don't. No matter how good your stuff, you must not look back. No matter how messy your stuff, never look back. Fixing a flub to feel better is not worth stopping. Don't edit as you go. Only forward! Looking back is a trap.

You will fix it later. What the Talking Draft Method gives you fast is spaghetti on the wall that you can rewrite, rewrite, rewrite -- later…once you're done with your first draft. In the meantime, don't edit as you go. And if you're transcribing, don't look at the output.

"The first draft of the script is always not good. But that's okay…
Be wrong as fast as you can."

- Andrew Stanton

There is scientifically proven neuroscience behind this idea. Technically speaking, we do not want to engage the portions of our brain's pre-frontal cortex that self-censors. If we deny that urge long enough, we will transcend the urge completely – this is how artists achieve a state of creative flow.

To have the end result of your dictation feel like a properly uniform story, it is preferable to move at the pace of the scenes as they play in your mind's eye. When a Talking Draft is done right, your first draft can be completed in nearly the same number of minutes as the runtime. But this is only if you can get going and stay going.

GET GOING, STAY GOING

Dictating a story for the stage or screen with The Talking Draft Method improves upon dictation with standard speech-to-text software. Anyone who has ever tried to write a stageplay or screenplay knows that it is a different form of writing than anything in a narrative style. It is partly a mechanical blueprint for production, and yet, there are portions where the dialogue and action lines should have the lyricism and carefully artful language of poetry.

A writer of screenplays or stageplays who achieves a creative flow state during the act of creation likely does so by limiting their narration to just those most artful elements, leaving for later the crude mechanics of location slug lines, parentheticals, transitions, etc.

Obviously, dictating a stageplay or a screenplay is different than dictating a novel or essay, and yet, most screenplay dictation tools fail to customize the experience specifically for the playwright or screenwriter.

No screenwriter wants the added bother of saying transitions aloud like "intercut with," or those annoying parentheticals like "into phone." These purely mechanical addendums should be added later in revisions.

No storyteller could naturally say something as artless and clunky as a location slug: "I-N-T, period, police dispatch office, dash, night." It is not helpful to have to say any mechanical elements aloud at all. Script elements like location slugs are so structural and unnatural compared to the ideal state of an artful raconteur telling a story, that dictating these things utterly spoils the experience of storytelling. Their disruptive nature actively inhibits creative flow.

A storyteller who wants to get the first draft of the script out of their head quickly does not want to utter clunky voice commands like "tab, tab" or "character name" or "Rebecca says" or anything else that bucks them out of their creative zone or knocks them off their story's pace.

The unwritten movie scene that writers imagine in their minds do not have an endless cacophony of "Jim says," "Judy says" before each dialogue line.

Considering that the goal at this Talking Draft stage is to achieve a state where your creativity is flowing freely, the ideal approach to dictation (the approach which will best facilitate high focus and low distractions) centers your narration solely on the creative elements, not the mechanical ones.

The easiest way to do this is to simply imagine the scene – with you as a fly on the wall, as if you're taking dictation from your characters.

Then, on "action" lines, describe the characters' movements in the style of an Audio Description service for the blind (where during pauses in dialogue a narrator provides concise yet vivid descriptions of a film or episode's visual elements that are essential to understanding the plot).

If you find yourself unsure about what the dialogue should be, do not worry, do not stop. Instead, your characters can literally say aloud in their dialogue things that the scene should eventually accomplish in later drafts. Your characters can say aloud the subtext even, as if reminding you of the story points that you need to work on in your revisions.

"The first draft is just you telling yourself the story."

- Terry Pratchett

When your characters are collaborating with you, the above quotation is literally true. Sometimes this technique may feel like your characters are helping you write the story as they "mark" their delivery and physical business here in the zero draft. That is perfectly fine. Whatever you need to do to get going and stay going – you will be okay. The goal in the Talking Draft is to get as much of the vitals out of your mind and into the script as fast as you can. The goal is to get it done.

The best way to do that is in a flow state. But what exactly is that?

Writing In a Flow State

The term "flow state" describes a mental state in which a person is completely immersed, absorbed, engrossed, and focused on a single task or activity. They are directing all of their attention toward the task. A person "in flow" may not notice time passing, think about why they are doing the task, or judge their efforts. Instead, they remain completely focused.

According to psychologist Mihaly Csíkszentmihályi who coined the term, "the ego falls away. Time flies. Every action, movement, and thought follows inevitably from the previous one, like playing jazz. Your whole being is involved, and you're using your skills to the utmost."

The flow state is the gold standard of work efficiency. Where there is flow, there is high productivity. When you are in a flow state you create more effortlessly. Sometimes the work is pulling details from many parts of your memory with fluid ease, but the work is always high in volume. This is the ideal state for writing our first drafts.

People describe a sense of fluidity between their task and mind, where they are totally absorbed by and deeply focused on something, beyond the point of distraction. Their senses are heightened. They are at one with the activity, as action and awareness sync to create an effortless momentum. It's true that the perception of time becomes hazy. Some people describe this feeling as being "in the zone." This is the flow state and it's accessible to everyone.

The Talking Draft Method is the one writing technique that comprises most of the best-known positive triggers while also eliminating the best-known blocks to achieving a flow state. Simply, no other writing style will set off a flow state session with greater regularity than the Talking Draft Method.

A musician who plays music in flow will sometimes remark that it feels like the music has become a part of them, and they are a part of the music. They don't become a conduit for some otherworldly songster, they become the music.

If you think of flow in terms of dance, flow is when your body moves in sync with the music because it is as if you are dancing <u>with</u> the music. Not "to" the music. Your body is the visualization of music. That is flow.

According to Csíkszentmihályi in his book *Finding Flow: The Psychology of Engagement with Everyday Life*, there are ten factors that accompany the flow experience. Flow experiences can occur in different ways for different people. While many of these factors may be present, it is not necessary to experience all of them for flow to occur:

1. The activity is intrinsically rewarding.

2. There are clear goals that, while challenging, are still attainable.

3. There is a complete focus on the activity itself.

4. People experience feelings of personal control over the situation and the outcome.

5. People feel serenity and a loss of self-consciousness.

6. There is immediate feedback.

7. People know that the task is doable and there is a balance between skill level and the challenge presented.

8. People experience a lack of awareness of their physical needs.

9. There is strong concentration and focused attention.

10. People experience a distorted sense of time, feeling so focused on the present that you lose track of time passing.

Flow has similarities with mindfulness, as both mental states focus on the present moment. However, people often use the term "flow" in reference to situations where they are being highly productive, whereas a person can be in a state of mindfulness regardless of whether they are doing a task.

Flow also has important differences with a slightly similar phenomenon called hyperfocus. Hyperfocus is often a characteristic of attention-deficit hyperactivity disorder (ADHD). Hyperfocus requires a person to be highly interested in or obsessed with the tasks, while flow can happen with almost any task that a person finds challenging, engaging, or rewarding.

Of the ten factors listed by Csíkszentmihályi, the tasks that tend to most encourage a state of flow are tasks that are challenging, but not impossible. They are rewarding, so that a person gets a sense of pleasure or purpose from doing it. And the tasks are in-depth, involving an investment of time or energy to make progress.

The flow state is often associated with the creative arts, such as painting, or music, but it's also been seen with brain surgeons and other highly technical tasks. When it occurs in a sport, people tend to call it being "in the zone." The act of creative writing within a defined structure like the screenplay format, and with specific page or scene targets, makes screenwriting in the Talking Draft Method a prime activity whose conditions are especially suited for achieving flow.

Your Brain In Flow

Dr. Charles J. Limb, MD has studied creativity and the brain at the National Institutes of Health and Johns Hopkins University School of Medicine. In recent years, his team went looking to understand the neuroscience behind the psychological and philosophical idea of the flow state.

Dr. Limb used functional MRI machines to watch the blood oxygen level of brain areas while patients were actively creative. One model used in this study was musical improvisation.

He found that when musicians improvise in a flow state, inside the musician's brain, an area that is thought to be involved in self-monitoring and self-consciousness turns off. At the same time, a different area that's thought to be autobiographical turns on. Language areas also turn on, and areas associated with self-expression turn on.

The scientist's hypothesis is that to be creative, we require a kind of dissociation where a big area of our brains shut off so that we're more uninhibited, willing to make mistakes, without constantly nullifying our generative impulses. This key condition to creativity boils down to the adage that we must not edit while we write.

Our generative impulses – i.e. new additive ideas – must not be second-guessed by our self-monitoring brain nor our self-conscious brain. Any new idea must not be fretted over and nit-picked. Instead, each new thought must be allowed to exist and we should quickly continue on to the next idea. For writers who are hard on themselves, this can be difficult, but it is absolutely vital. We must stop editing ourselves while creating!

"Get the goop out first, then organize."

- Screenwriter Alvin Sargent

Once our brains start generating new ideas, more new ideas will come because we will unconsciously feel a slight rush of satisfaction after each act of creation. These neurochemical rushes actually help generate the next clear thought. But for any of this flowing creativity to begin we must first not say "no" to ourselves. One of the laws of improv is "yes, and" - this philosophy applies to all flow state creativity.

Dr. Limb's team also used freestyle rappers in his test and found that with eyes closed, while freestyling, the visual centers of the rapper's brain lit up as brightly as the language centers. This suggested to Dr. Limb's team that the creative focus required to improvise spoken language was similar to that of the musician with his keyboard, but with even more activity. It seems spoken language improv was kickstarted by visual stimuli - imagined visual stimuli - but visual cues nonetheless.

When both the pianist and the rapper emerged from the fMRI machines, they felt exhilarated from their creative bursts and had lost track of time. When we come out of a flow state, the first thing we usually do is check what time it is. That's because a truly immersive creative experience shuts down one of the parts of the brain having to do with our brain consciously monitoring ourselves and thus general temporality.

Dr. Limb's tentative conclusion is hopeful: Artistic creativity is a neurologic product that can be examined using rigorous scientific methods. It's magical but it's not magic. We can maximize the conditions that generate flow state creativity and minimize the factors which disrupt it. The primary element for flow is to focus.

IMPROVE FOCUS TO FLOW

Flow requires very high focus of attention. Improving your focus takes time. The first step is to confront the reasons behind your distractions and come up with a method to confront and defeat your distractions.

First, resist the urge to multitask whenever you seek to enter into a flow state. When you are starting this process of flow state training, you might benefit from limiting any sensory triggers. As you get better, you can add them back. For some, this may mean that when you're beginning to improve your focus, you could try selective deprivations such as writing at night or noise cancelling headphones.

Eventually your strength of focus will be such that you will be able to flow in completely normal conditions. However, other factors will remain important to limit even when you are expert at slipping into high focus flow. At the top of this list is the need to resist the urge to edit yourself.

Editing, polishing, tweaking, spelling, grammar, all of the fine-tuning of language, and syntax is for later passes. When you get going, you must keep going. This is paramount: no distractions, no revisions.

Any time a writer manually types any sentence into a script document, they can also instantly re-read that line and instantly begin to think of the hundred other ways to say the line. Whenever we type, we also make it too easy to edit. Editing is the enemy. Any editing or any self-criticism activates the exact part of the brain that we actually need to turn off if we want to reach a flow state. We do not want any of this friction. The freedom to reconsider, rewrite, or delay is friction – not flow.

For this reason, the act of typing itself can be hinderance to flow state creativity because of common typos that are unavoidable. Each typo is like a thorn underfoot that pricks us out of the zone. These moments of sharp discomfort severely interrupt the preferred state of acceptance and surrender that is required for the flow state. The Talking Draft Method avoids this problem altogether by not showing your speech-to-text engine's text output by default.

Many people report that getting into a flow state is all about moving with intention, at peak focus and relaxation, letting go of any self-censorship, surrendering to embody the task. It sounds a little metaphysical – like an athlete who wants to "be the ball," or a dancer who wants to "feel the music," but it's true. Storytellers have to try to become one with the story. No distance, no distraction, and no doubt.

To achieve this, you have to commit to eliminating "the hundred other good ideas" and just keep moving forward until you're gliding along with seemingly no effort at all. Do not doubt your ideas, become one with them, frictionless.

A truly immersive creative experience requires your full attention. If we understand the specific things that kick us out of our flow, we can eliminate them. Also, we can consciously nurture the nature of our personal way into flow. These engineered writing conditions will help get us back into the headspace of flow easier and easier.

With targeted effort, writers can effectively hotwire the flow state, acclimating ourselves to learn how to slip into the zone more easily. All you have to do is pay attention to the things that get you in the zone.

Find Your Way In

We all experience the flow state of mind from time to time. But few of us can get in the zone whenever we want to. It takes some controlled conditions to achieve "flow" regularly. It can be learned.

It takes approximately 10 to 15 minutes of focused attention to reach a flow state. Once in flow state, your experience in it may last from 30 minutes to several hours. It is also possible to achieve flow more than one time per day, given the right conditions.

What it takes to bring about flow varies from person to person. It might be as simple as turning off your phone. Organizing workspace can be immensely helpful, as might judiciously cluttering your workspace.

For most people, eliminating distractions is vital.

For most people recent exercise and adrenaline is very helpful.

Commonly, writers find that they tell stories better to someone, this phenomenon might be because of the dopamine hit with adrenaline that comes from live performance. You can replicate this brain chemistry if you've recently taken a light jog or if you do a Talking Draft while pacing around the room, imagining yourself telling the story to an audience.

Some users of the Talking Draft Method record video of themselves and post it later to the internet. This trick, of a potential audience may be enough to generate a steady amount of performance-induced adrenaline. These are the kinds of mind-hacks that professional athletes and musicians take for granted and which writers may need to synthesize.

Short of simulating a performance posture, we can also program our minds with flow state triggers that are more passive in nature. Common ones include a consistent scent of candle, or a go-to set of comfortable clothing like heavy socks or heavy blanket, or a specific piece of wordless music playing lightly in the background.

By consciously adding these positively triggering stimuli to our work space, we build working conditions so that when there are *hopefully* episodes of flow, our minds will subconsciously associate the trigger stimuli with those periods of high focus and flow. Going forward, those smells, sounds, or sensations will prepare our minds for the work mode that enables flow state.

Reaching a flow state isn't a magical or illusive mindset. Anyone can get there, and practice helps us get there more quickly.

You know you've prepared yourself adequately when you don't have to think about ignoring distractions; you ignore them with little effort. Ultimately, you are so focused on the task at hand that the rest of the world fades away. The result is a blend of happiness and peak performance that is nearly impossible to experience without finding the task hugely satisfying.

The more you write for the flow state, the easier it is to get into a flow state so that you can create your best writing. A flow state is when you are able to write without thinking about what you are doing. The words flow effortlessly onto the page. You are one with your writing. Your sense of self and sense of time dissolve away, you harmonize with the task.

When writers get to a flow state, it feels like you're in your own little bubble, your own creative world, and no amount of distraction can divert you from what you're doing. You are present. Hours fly by without you realizing it. You look up from your desk only to notice the sun has set. Congratulations, you will probably need a lot of electrolytes and potassium, but you will surely feel ecstatic. Now that you're done, you can begin.

"No one's stuff is right immediately...
It's gonna be terrible before it's not. And that's okay."

-Ava DuVernay

It should help relieve pressure from yourself to remember that all scripts are rewritten many times, but it is impossible to rewrite a blank page. The first draft does not need to be perfect, but it does need to be done. For this reason, a flow state generated by the Talking Draft Method is the absolute best way to create a first draft fast.

How to Flow

In his book defining flow, Csíkszentmihályi explains that there are some specific strategies you can use to help set the stage for entering a flow state. Each of these is aided by use of the Talking Draft Method.

Set Clear Goals

A flow state is likely to occur when an individual is faced with a task that has clear goals that require specific responses. Finishing a certain number of scenes in one sitting, whether it be a feature's worth or one episode is a good example of when a flow state might occur. For the duration of the writing session, the writer has very specific goals and a set procedure of scene descriptions to flesh-out, allowing attention to be focused entirely on the improvisation of dialog and action for each scene in the outline.

Eliminate Distractions

It's more difficult to experience flow if there are things in your environment competing for your attention. The Talking Draft Method reduces the distractions that come with typing so you can fully focus on the task at hand. You might also wear noise-canceling headphones or play wordless music that is evocative of the story that you're telling. Mainly, by not seeing the most recent typo – and by not having to think about grammar rules or spelling, you free your prefrontal cortex to turn off and let the language center, visual, and expression regions of the brain take over.

Add an Element of Challenge

"Flow also happens when a person's skills are fully involved in overcoming a challenge that is just about manageable, so it acts as a magnet for learning new skills and increasing challenges," Csíkszentmihályi explains. "If challenges are too low, one gets back to flow by increasing them. If challenges are too great, one can return to the flow state by learning new skills." Creating an outline that tells the whole story is the first part of the challenge, you establish a benchmark of completion. Talking the first draft in one sitting is the ultimate challenge.

Practice Meditation and Mindfulness

Meditation and mindfulness may help us get into a flow state more easily. Mindfulness involves becoming more attuned to the present moment. One study found that practicing mindfulness helped athletes experience a flow state and improved their performance. Meditation generates an increase in the activity of dopamine (a brain chemical involved in pleasure and motivation), and other studies show that this chemical is produced when people are experiencing flow. One can prime the pump for the other; Using the Talking Draft Method after meditation, after exercise, or during exercise is the best possible condition. A 2021 review paper suggested that the brain's locus coeruleus-norepinephrine system, which helps regulate control over engaging or disengaging tasks in response to stimuli, is activated by flow state activities – in other words, getting into flow keeps us in flow. But exercise also releases norepinephrine just the same as being in flow - the chemical clears the runway for flow.

Choose a Pursuit You Enjoy

You aren't likely to achieve flow if you are engaged in an activity you dislike. A writer using the Talking Draft Method to finish her first draft is free to focus on achieving creative flow more than if she sat down to type it. The reason is psychological: Most first drafts don't get finished because the old style of typing a first draft is fraught with all of the snags and thorns that prevent us from achieving the peak productivity that comes with flow. Writers even grow frustrated with the "uncooperative" story. With the Talking Draft Method, writers avoid the many friction points inherent in tedious written drafts. Writers who use the Talking Draft Method are less likely to fall into the "First Draft Trap."

ALL ABOUT OUTLINES

After the trap of "trying to edit while they write," the second largest reason writers give up finishing their first drafts is that people skimp on the outline.

Outlines are key. It is not uncommon to spend most of your time on the task of outlining while making a first draft.

The more you are able to troubleshoot your outline, eliminating holes in logic, building in believable character growth, plotting organic setbacks, twists, reveals, and also pacing these moments so that the overall step-outline has a big, memorable moment every few pages, the better your eventual draft will be.

Without an outline, some writers discover plot holes too late. Without an outline, usually the first quarter of the story will shine while thereafter, the quality drops off with every page (See: infamous underdrawn horse).

A plot hole is usually catastrophic for a writer who is trying to finish her first draft because at one level, any story is a piece of logic: Character A does X to character B which causes Y for character C who does Z in response. The sequence of actions and choices have to make sense, both as a chain of events and as a series of choices that real, evolving characters would make in response to those events.

As a writer, if you ever find yourself making major logic changes while writing, steering the story in a new direction, then your overall trajectory is at risk for veering off the mark. The result of writing in this manner will likely leave your story in a very different place than where you thought you were aiming. A script that has these features can often read as meandering. Often the finale seems to "come out of nowhere," and the story nearly always leaves some secondary characters' choices as appearing arbitrary.

There are exceptions, of course. The meandering could all end up as a happy accident of a masterpiece. But most often, a writer who has not plotted the story ahead of time with an outline, and checked it closely in order to verify that there are no plot holes, will usually fail. They fail because they usually just stop writing as soon as they encounter a plot hole too big to cross.

You can choose to write this way, knowing that you may write yourself into a hole and continue to write as you plunge deeper into an unknown abyss. Whenever you finally decide you stop your descent, or decide that the story is done, you may find that overall your first draft was a waste of time and effort. This is the case with between 85% and 90% of storytellers according to the NaNoWriMo surveys. It hurts.

Outlines are the solution. They always help. The Talking Draft Method works wonders if you do like Howard Hawks did when he invented the technique and you begin telling your story with a tight outline guiding you.

This is the reason that TV showrunners and film studios which contract with writers for screenplays often require outlines as the first step. A good outline will save everyone mountains of frustration and pain. The business of screenwriting is simply not made for "pantsers" (i.e. someone who writes with no outline, "by the seat of their pants").

People who hope to become professional writers likely need to abandon the romantic notion of letting the story lead you, or "discovering the story" with your characters. Writing for a living is a serious job with consequences for failure to deliver. Most buyers want outlines.

If you're serious about becoming a professional writer, you must impose deadlines on yourself as soon as possible because the first time you successfully land a real writing job, you will have contracted deadlines. All buyers have deadlines. You are legally bound to deliver the goods on time with a professional polish.

Even when writing your own specs (a "speculative" or non-commissioned screenplay) it is wise to set a twelve-week deadline for yourself and get good at beating that deadline. This is training for the day when a professional opportunity arrives.

Writers Guild of America contracts specify screenwriters have a minimum of twelve weeks to produce the first draft of a script - but it is not unheard of that some contracts are as short as eight weeks.

You should anticipate that the producer or executive will begin calling your agent, manager, or you in about four weeks – sniffing around to see how you are progressing, hoping for a page count or maybe to "see some pages."

Usually the contract is negotiated with "steps" built in. The first draft…is a step. The first rewrite is another step. Each of these steps has a deadline and a fee that you are paid. But many contracts also include an outline or story treatment as the first step.

How to Outline

The first thing you need to know is that a bad story often looks like the infamous "underdrawn horse" of the pantser:

As you can see in the illustration, the first part of the story is well formed, with great details and depth – Act 1 is usually just peachy. Then in the middle section, rather than specific and focused writing, we have "stuff" and the quality drops dramatically. Until in the end, well, we often just try to wrap it up – and here the illustration turns into a toddler's stick figure. What is even supposed to be a horse? Who cares…end.

It's a cute meme, but the idea behind it is powerfully true. Writing without an outline will very often lead to the underdrawn horse. This is what we practice to avoid.

The easiest way to write an outline is with a two-stage method. The first stage is the general big picture view – often called the beat sheet -- and the second stage is your scene-by-scene outline that fleshes out the big picture view by adding a location-by-location list of scene cues, defining the vital action that takes place in each scene location. This more detailed, micro scale of all the scenes is often called the step-outline.

What is a Beat Sheet & How to Start

A beat sheet is the abbreviated precursor to a scene-by-scene outline.

The beat sheet identifies just the big important moments in a film or episode and also lays out what should generally happen in each Act of the story. Your beat sheet is the high-level, general, macro view of your story – 10,000 feet above the nitty-gritty.

Start by keeping your mind at the macro scale, and in one sentence, define the large "sections" of your story.

The free story outliner at www.TalkingDraft.com allows you to outline at this macro level according to different popular story models. The macro-level beat sheet also generates page targets to tell you how long these various "sections" should be (depending on what structure you select and how long you want your script to be in the end).

These are not - repeat NOT – unbreakable rules. Your beat sheet's page target reminders will hopefully help your story keep its shape and balance. Because in screenplays every page is one minute, the approximate page targets will help prevent later sections in your story from being too thin, and resulting in the underdrawn horse.

Additionally, the section page targets at www.TalkingDraft.com should keep you from rambling too long when the mic is on. In fact, with a moderate amount of outline planning, the Talking Draft Method can carry you from your beat sheet to your first draft in one sitting.

Let's explore outlines with the movie *The Wizard of Oz*. It helps to begin by defining the beginning, middle, and end of your story. One sentence each. This is the most macro view possible of your idea. The basic beginning, middle, and end of *The Wizard of Oz* might look like this:

Beginning

```
Dorothy is a misfit in Kansas before a tornado hits which
sends her to Oz.
```

Middle

```
Dorothy and her new friends, the Scarecrow, Tinman, and
Cowardly Lion, arrive in the Emerald City where the Wizard
of Oz tells them he will grant their wishes if they kill the
Wicked Witch of the West.
```

End

```
Dorothy awakens back home in Kansas, surrounded by, and with
a new appreciation for, her loved ones.
```

The reason it is important to know the <u>middle</u> and <u>end</u> of your story before you begin is because if we are not very familiar with those latter two things, there is a higher likelihood of writing the underdrawn horse.

The most simple and famous story structure in the western tradition is by Ancient Greek genius Aristotle who defined four pillars of a story:

1. **Stasis** - The introduction / story setup.
2. **Thesis** - The rising action / the stakes get higher.
3. **Antithesis** - The crisis / falling action.
4. **Synthesis** - The climax / the resolution.

The second and third pillars of an Aristotelian story are usually combined into what most people think of as the "middle." In other words, the second act has two parts, 2A (rising action) and 2B (falling action). Therefore, in order to create a proper Aristotelian 4-Act beat sheet for *The Wizard of Oz*, from the basics above, one needs only to split the "middle" into two sections at a key plot point. Some writers call this key scene "The Threshold," others, "The Midpoint."

In *The Wizard of Oz*, this moment arises when The Wizard sends Dorothy on a mission to steal the Witch's broomstick. Knowing that, a proper 4-Act beat sheet for *The Wizard of Oz* would look like this:

Act 1 – Stasis

The introduction / story setup.

In Kansas, Dorothy doesn't fit in. She gets in trouble and gets in the way. To save her dog from the mean neighbor, Dorothy runs away. A traveling fortune teller tricks her into going back home. She returns as a tornado hits the farm; she is knocked unconscious. The house flies - it crashes in Munchkinland killing The Wicked Witch of the East. The Good Witch of the North calls Dorothy a hero. The Wicked Witch of the West tries to claim her dead sister's magic ruby slippers, but Dorothy has them. The Wicked Witch swears revenge. The Good Witch tells Dorothy to follow the Yellow Brick Road to Emerald City where she can ask the Wizard of Oz to help her return home.

Act 2 – Thesis

The rising action / the stakes get higher.

On her journey, Dorothy meets the Scarecrow, who wants a brain; the Tin Man, who seeks a heart; and the Cowardly Lion, who desires courage. She invites them to accompany her and ask the Wizard for what they lack. Despite the Witch's attempts to stop them with sleeping spells and other magic, they reach the city and see the Wizard, who appears as a giant ghostly head.

Act 3 – Antithesis

The crisis / falling action.

The Wizard agrees to grant their requests but he gives them an impossible task to defeat the Wicked Witch because The feared Witch followed her to Oz. Panic sweeps through his city. Self-doubt creeps in among everyone. Shortly after starting for the Witch's castle, Dorothy is captured by the Witch. "I'm frightened, Auntie Em!" she cries in the dungeon where she simply wants to be home again.

Act 4 – Synthesis

The climax / the resolution.

Toto escapes. Dorothy's friends save her, and together they defeat the Witch, but the Wizard is revealed to be a fraud whose balloon flew him to Oz. Nevertheless, Dorothy gets home.

MACRO – MICRO

When writing the macro view, the 10,000-foot perspective of your beat sheet, brevity is key. You want to include just enough details that you will remember the kinds of gambits which the whole section will eventually include, but not so many specifics that you get bogged down in small details.

On www.TalkingDraft.com the section description areas for your typing are truncated for this reason (although you can click-and-drag the corner of the text area with your mouse or finger to make them bigger).

After your macro-scale beat sheet is done, then you can begin fleshing-out those sections into a scene-by-scene outline. Here we begin drilling down into the micro view of the plot. Mindful of the underdrawn horse, you might begin by fleshing out the too-thin description for Act 4 of *The Wizard of Oz* in the preceding example, and come up with a list of scenes:

"Toto escapes from the dungeon and leads her three friends to the castle. They ambush three guards, don their uniforms, and free Dorothy. The Witch sets fire to the Scarecrow, so Dorothy tosses a bucket of water on him, inadvertently splashing the Witch who melts and disappears. Dorothy brings the Witch's broomstick to the Wizard, who is revealed to be a carnival showman whose hot air balloon brought him to the Emerald City by accident, he agrees to take Dorothy home in his balloon. He leaves the Scarecrow in charge of Emerald City, with the Tin Man and the Lion as his aides. Toto leaps from Dorothy's arms, Dorothy goes after him, missing the balloon. Glinda instructs Dorothy how to use the magic slippers to get home, she does. She wakes up in her bedroom, surrounded by her family and friends."

Each of the above sentences could be its own scene. In fact, that <u>is</u> each key scene in Act 4 of *The Wizard of Oz*. That is how short your individual scene descriptions can be. These are just notes to yourself.

As you add these individual micro-level scenes to your scene-by-scene outline (creating what some call a "step-outline") you can simply type the location slug into the scene's location field. Like this exterior shot:

```
EXT. MUNCHKINLAND - DAY
```

When describing what happens in this colorful location, the detail specificity in your step-outline increases from the beat sheet's macro-10,000-foot view, to a micro-100-foot view. With brevity, add each scene description to your outline.

Remember, your outline serves to remind you only of the vitals: precisely what the scene needs to accomplish…or exactly what a character needs to discover in that specific location.

"You should be able to tell any good story in two or three lines."

- Screenwriter Richard Matheson

At the end, you should be able to read all of your scene descriptions in order and have it sound like a very concise story. Brevity is key.

For example, the first (micro) scene of the Aristotelian 2nd Act in *Wizard of Oz* could be written as simply as:

"Dorothy takes her first steps down the yellow brick road singing."

From that simple reminder, a writer can use the Talking Draft Method to describe the jaunty action and dialogue (and/or lyrics).

When you're done with that scene, simply move on to the next one. Repeat until you're done.

With a moderate amount of outline planning, the Talking Draft Method can carry you from your beat sheet to your first draft in one sitting. This is the goal of the Talking Draft Method.

WHAT

STORY STRUCTURES FOR OUTLINING

In addition to the Aristotelian basis of western storytelling, a few other guides will all contribute to a better understanding of how story works in a screenplay. These are included here for you to consider.

Over time, there have been several popular story theorists and screenwriting gurus who have taught slightly different outlining techniques. TalkingDraft.com guides you to write a beat sheet using a guru's method of your choice. Of course, you can also write your outline "freeform" where the only thing that guides you is a logline. The simplest story structure is from Aristotle who taught that stories had 4 Acts that move a hero through a rise and fall.

But no matter how complex your story model, the beat sheet is how you start your outline. You first identify the key plot points and place them roughly in the correct area of your story. This gives you guideposts to navigate your writing through the fog of uncertainty that all writers face. These guideposts, or key beats, help keep you on track and on pace.

Story structure is hard. Just like music theory is hard. Anyone who has ever tried to write a screenplay or play freestyle jazz knows this.

For most aspiring screenwriters, it helps to learn structures. The goal could be that you learn them so well that you can forget about the guidelines and allow your story to come out freely. And yet, because what you studied is so deeply embedded in your sense of story, you will find that intuitively your story will begin to take on an organic and pleasingly balanced shape. That might be a goal for some. Many veteran writers describe their work that way.

Jazz Saxophonist John Coltrane was a master of music theory. With a perfect ear, he knew all the laws of harmonics and musical scales intimately. Far beyond memorization, these mathematical formulas were in the marrow of his bones. Knowing those rules allowed him to freestyle in and around the melody and rhythm.

Great screenwriters are like this. Their stories don't scream formula or structure but they do have a pleasing shape. That shape organically fits the story, the shape supports the character moments that the story is begging for us to see. It has been said that the better you are as a screenwriter, the better you are at hiding your structure. But when you're really great, there is no "hiding" – all the elements will harmonize organically and be appreciated by those who understand story craft.

This is not to suggest that structure doesn't matter. Structure absolutely matters, but structure is not formula.

Advanced Screenwriting

Not all stories have the same shape. Honest screenwriting coaches will tell you that a great screenplay can break all the "rules" of structure. Many writers who set out to follow all the rules likely hamstring their creativity. A plot point in your favorite movie very well may come 10-20-30 pages too "late" and still work.

There is no magic formula. Don't feel like you have to hack off parts of your story in order to fit it into one of the story structures available in this book's Appendix. Any story worth caring about is unique. You want readers to care about your story.

The upside of following an established screenplay structure is that if you follow one of these guides, you <u>will</u> get a completed script. That's good. That's especially good for aspiring writers who *need* to finish their first several screenplays. Especially since we know that most aspiring writers don't finish even one.

This is especially true if we are honest with ourselves and just accept that the first draft is probably going to stink. Most first drafts are bad. That's okay. If we still love the story once we're done with our Talking Draft, we will surely care enough to start the hard work of rewriting, reworking, and getting notes from friends and colleagues. Version after draft, after revision, cuts after adds, until the script is finally ready for eyes that matter.

This is the path that will lead you to having more completed screenplays. And because we will only hone our voice and our feel for story shape by doing, by revising, by reworking our own words, this is the path that will get us good faster.

The downside of following a story structure to a tee is that it may not be compelling or unique.

A creative chef likely does not want to follow a cookie cutter one-size-fits-all recipe, they may want to experiment. But aspiring chefs should learn the basics enough to at least get the food chemistry right. But go right head and see what happens when you use fewer eggs; you might not get fluffy brownies, but you may find yourself with a nice fudgy one. Perhaps fudge suits your story.

Experimentation is fun for people who have time to play with. But if you don't feel like you have time to dither, perhaps approaching your work with a bit more of a regimented mindset may help you to get proficient faster. The faster you are proficient, the faster you will be good.

This book is predicated on the idea that a <u>fast</u> first draft is beneficial because most people don't finish their first drafts, and so they sadly never get the opportunity to do the real work of rewriting and revising.

This book stresses outlines because a structured story is more likely to get finished. This book suggests using model beat sheets when outlining because they are helpful for beginners and will give you the chance to pre-address notes and troubleshoot your story. This book teaches the Talking Draft Method because it is the fastest way to generate a first draft.

Your first draft is the goal of this book. But finishing your first draft is not the end of your journey – it is only the beginning of the dozens of rewrites that every script needs. Are we ready to start?!

Not Formulas

As Aristotle established, we often begin a story by painting a quick and basic understanding of the world before the tumultuous events of the plot. This introduction or "setup" is a quick establishment of a state of equilibrium (the stasis). Soon, a theme emerges, or an argument posited by something revealed by the plot (the thesis). As the main character moves forward, it's like the world has grown or changed, the hero's perceptions of the theme are then challenged during the third act (the antithesis), until the hero finally overcomes their peril by using all they've learned to find a final solution that brings them, changed for the better, to a new place of emotional clarity (the synthesis).

This shape isn't unique to screenwriting; every story ever told around a campfire follows some sort of structure, with a beginning, middle and end. But screenplays are extraordinarily structure-driven.

By design, screenplays have only a specific number of minutes (and therefore pages) to accomplish a ton.

You must introduce your characters, their world, you add new people to the world, you blow that world up, reassemble it thanks to the power of friendship or a MacGuffin and tie up all loose ends before the lights come back on and the audience heads home.

The main characteristic of screenwriting is the economy of storytelling on display. Action lines cannot be too long but they also must be extremely evocative and communicate theme and tone at the same time. Action lines sometimes will sound like Haiku poetry.

Dialogue is concise and yet human. Screenwriters have to intertwine plot and character so tightly that everything else is secondary to that goal.

Action, dialogue, even the very syntax of word choice is woven tighter than any other kind of writing and if any of it doesn't serve the structure, it has to be cut.

Many of the popular screenwriting structure guides in Hollywood are based on the work done by Sarah Lawrence College professor Joseph

Campbell's study of the ancient monomyth; A kind of proto story structure that has been reinforced by human storytelling since our earliest written example, *The Epic of Gilgamesh.*

This structure is sometimes called "The Hero's Journey." Campbell was not suggesting that all stories have to follow the model, but that if we take a random story and line it up to the major sections of the monomyth, we will see places where the story will often turn as predicted, and that those turns *feel* as if they come at the right time. Many suggest that humans have conditioned ourselves over hundreds of thousands of years of storytelling to *feel* a good story innately.

When outlining a story, it helps to model your work-in-progress on one of the following structures. But remember, though the screenplay form is extremely regimented, the different outline structures found in this book's Appendix are suggestions, not prescriptions.

However, if you are a novice screenwriter, or one of the many who have not finished a screenplay, do try sticking to a structure at first. Get your first draft finished, then begin the work of rewriting.

Many of the popular Hollywood screenplay structures even go so far as to suggest specific pages / story percentages for when some of the guideposts should hit. However, in this book we will leave those prescriptions aside for now (though they are available in the beat sheet calculator in www.TalkingDraft.com's free script outliner).

These structures are suggestions, not laws. The ability to disguise your structure inside an organic narrative comes with practice. Aspiring writers and film students are often encouraged to lightly use guidance structures so as to acclimate themselves to the pacing of a balanced film.

Soon, upon fully understanding the reasons for the pacing of screenwriting structures, you will feel comfortable coloring outside the lines as you make the story completely your own.

STC

Screenwriter Blake Snyder taught how to shape a story with 15 beats in his *Save the Cat* books. Some of Blake's "beats" are long sections, while other beats are short, specific key moments. The following is Blake's popular structure and how he would outline *The Wizard of Oz*.

Opening Image

The opening scene sets the tone, mood, type, and scope of the project. It's a 'before' snapshot of the hero and world.

```
Dorothy and Toto in Kansas running away from a problem.
```

Set-up

A sequence of many scenes introduces the key characters and character flaws that need fixing. You might also set up the stakes and goal.

```
Her family has no time for her, she feels she doesn't belong.
Her neighbor wants to kill her dog. Dorothy runs away, meets
a fortune teller who says to go home.
```

Theme Stated

In a single scene during setup, a character may pose a question that forms the theme of the story, or a location might suggest the story's theme.

```
Auntie Em says Dorothy should find somewhere to stay out of
the way and out of trouble. (Is it somewhere over the rainbow?)
```

Catalyst

In one first act scene, a life-changing event, often bad news or a "Call to Adventure," makes the main character realize that Stasis = Death.

```
Tornado hits, she's knocked unconscious.
```

Debate

A section of several scenes where the hero reacts to the change that's occurred. The main character makes a choice.

```
Is she in Kansas? Is this where she can find happiness? How
can she escape Oz? Where is the Wizard?
```

Break into Act 2

In one scene, the hero leaves the old world behind and chooses something new. A strong, definite change as the story proper begins.

Dorothy takes her first steps down the yellow brick road.

B-Story

Often the 'love' story or introduction of new characters. This beat gives us a break from the tension of the main story; it is a subplot to help carry the theme of the story.

Dorothy's team comes together and overcomes their faults.

Fun & Games

The heart of the story, this fulfills the promise of the poster. The stakes are not too high yet, the hero is exploring the new world of Act 2.

The friends she meets along the way are revealed individually.

Midpoint

The momentary threshold between the first half and the second half of the story; the stakes are raised; the fun and games are over. It's sometimes a false success, or more often something goes badly wrong.

The Wizard gives them an impossible task: to defeat the Witch.

Bad Guys Close In

This section of the story is where the hero is really tested, the knife is twisted. Now a different challenge must be overcome. Perhaps the Bad guys regroup; or the hero's team unravels.

The Witch followed her. The city panics. Self-doubt creeps in.

All is Lost

In one moment it's clear the hero's life is in a shambles. There may be 'a whiff of death,' often if not physically, then symbolically. The old way of thinking dies. The hero may give up, there seems to be no hope.

Dorothy is captured by the Witch, "I'm frightened, Auntie Em!"

Dark Night of the Soul

The hero ruminates in the darkness before the dawn. Hero sometimes figures out the answer with insight from the B-Story.

In prison she simply wants to be home again.

Break into Act 3

The hero has dug deep, learned, changed, and found the solution. The stories carried by the theme and sub plot intertwine with the main plot. The hero has an idea to solve the problem and the end is in sight.

Toto Escapes. Her friends don't give up on Dorothy.

Finale

The final act is where new world is revealed. Perhaps the plan fails but the heroes improvise, the bad guys are dispatched, the problem is fixed.

The friends overcome their fears, storm the castle, kill the Witch. The Wizard is exposed. Glinda teaches Dorothy how to get home.

Final Image

The closing scene should be the opposite of the opening scene; it is the visual proof that change has occurred and is real.

Dorothy wakes, surrounded by her loved ones. Realizes "there's no place like home."

SYD FIELD

In his book *Screenplay*, Hollywood legend Syd Field lays out his version of the beat sheet and defines the sections. He uses a three act structure with a long 2nd Act. Here again is the *Wizard of Oz* as he would map it.

Act 1

A section where character and story setting are introduced.

We see Dorothy in her everyday world and see her running home to tell her aunt and uncle that Mrs. Gulch threatened her little dog, Toto.

Inciting Incident

A scene with the incident that kicks-off the story.

A tornado hits, but Dorothy doesn't make it back to the storm cellar in time because she is trying to find Toto. She's knocked out cold as the house flies away.

Plot Point 1

An incident, episode or event that hooks the action and spins it around in another direction

Dorothy wakes up in Oz, meets Glinda the Good Witch of the North who declares her a hero because she killed the Wicked Witch of the East. Glinda gives magic shoes to Dorothy and tells her to travel to the Emerald City to ask the Wizard of Oz for help to return to Kansas.

First Half of Act 2: Confrontation

A section of the story full of conflicts and attempts to reach a goal.

Some of the friends that Dorothy meets along the way are frightening, or frightened, but all of them eventually form one unit.

Pinch 1

The pinch is an action or an incident that concentrates the story toward the midpoint which comes next

Glinda the Good Witch cures the spell that had put Dorothy and her friends to sleep. Dorothy continues on to Oz.

Midpoint

An important scene in the middle of the script. Often a reversal of fortune or revelation that changes the direction of the story

Dorothy and her new friends, the Scarecrow, the Tinman and the Cowardly Lion, arrive in the Emerald City. Here they meet the Wizard of Oz, who tells them he will grant their wishes if they kill the Wicked Witch of the West.

Second Half of Act 2: Confrontation

During this section, conflict escalates and the stakes are raised

The Emerald City is terrified by The Wicked Witch who is hounding Dorothy.

Pinch 2

A scene comprising an action or an incident that concentrates the story toward the point which comes next

Dorothy and Toto are captured by the Wicked Witch of the West.

Plot Point 2

An event that thrusts the plot in a new direction, leading into a new act of the screenplay

Toto escapes and leads Dorothy's three friends to the castle. They ambush three guards, don their uniforms, and free Dorothy.

Act 3: Showdown Climax

The section of the story where forces in opposition confront each other and victory or defeat is the outcome

Dorothy melts the Wicked Witch with a bucket of water.

Resolution

A short section of Act 3 with the final conflict. Issues of the story will be resolved. Goals will be achieved or not achieved

Dorothy and her friends return to the Emerald City. They discover that the Wizard of Oz is a fraud, but he helps them anyway. The four friends discover that they had what they needed all along.

Denouement

A scene that reveals why it's okay to end the story here.

In the end, Dorothy awakens back home in Kansas, surrounded by (and with a new appreciation for) her loved ones.

Other popular screenwriting beat sheet guides can be found in this book's Appendix and at www.ScriptOutliner.com.

THE SOUND OF FLOW

Early in the rehearsal phase of a production there will often be a "Table Read" where the cast sits at a table along with one specialized reader who reads all stage directions or action lines.

This narrative reader will often skip over the parts of the scene description that describe emotional-states, elements which will surely be conveyed by the actor's delivery – but otherwise, the actors read their lines, skipping their dialog's emotional-state parentheticals.

The end result sounds like a radio drama. It usually takes only slightly longer than the runtime of the actual film.

Now imagine that one person reads all the dialogue lines (skipping parentheticals and character names), and she also reads every single action line or stage direction, including the action lines that specify a character's emotional state.

That is what it sounds like to perform a Talking Draft. This is exactly what it sounds like to hear Rod Serling create the first drafts of his *Twilight Zone* episodes on his old audio Dictabelts.

CLICK AS YOU GO

The last hurdle to a painless Talking Draft is the issue of what's called diarization: noting "who-says-what-when" in dialogue.

Most transcription software does not help screenwriters in this regard. They require you to go through a big block of transcribed text and manually break the paragraph of text into chunks according to who says what. That is a huge, unnecessary pain and it slows down the process to a grind.

Talking Draft experts found that manually notating your dictation for "who-says-what-when" *as you talk* is the best way to keep racing forward using the Talking Draft Method.

As you dictate your action lines and dialogue, you can diarize with one finger. Thanks to this innovation at www.TalkingDraft.com, one of Hollywood's best-kept secrets can become your own secret weapon.

You will diarize by tapping the number keys on your keyboard:

The number keys 1-9 correspond to the different speaking characters in your scene's dialogue.

Tap-and-release a number button 1-9. Then say *that* character's line.

Tap-and-release the zero key 0 before dictating an action line.

It is that easy.

When the transcriber is not recording, mouse-clicking one of the number buttons 1-9 will allow you to edit that button's name. Once you give a character name to a number, the name will appear in your script output.

Helpfully, the app at www.TalkingDraft.com allows you to replicate the character configuration from a previous scene. Adjusting it as necessary will help you keep your main characters' number keys consistent, this aids muscle-memory and will help you diarize without thinking about too much beyond the story in your mind's eye.

Whether you're a screenwriter or a playwright, what the Talking Draft Method does better than any other writing system is help you get your first draft done fast – like the speed of sound fast.

So if you believe that the first draft just needs to get finished, and you can trust yourself to fix your draft later, the Talking Draft Method saves you from most of the traps of a first draft because you get a beat sheet calculator and script outliner for free.

At any point, you can export your outline file from TalkingDraft.com into a word processor and type more words like it's the 1920s — OR, if you can picture the unwritten scenes in your head, we suggest you use the Talking Draft Method to transcribe your first draft because it's actually in fact the 2020s.

The Talking Draft webapp exports a file that all major screenwriting software can parse directly into screenplay format. You will open your screenplay for the first time to find a complete draft, even if it is just the spaghetti on the wall which you can rewrite, rewrite, rewrite.

"The first draft of anything is shit."

- Ernest Hemingway

It's harsh but true that the first draft doesn't need to be great, it just needs to get done. As Phoebe Waller-Bridge says: "You can always edit a bad page. You can't edit a blank page." From decades of experience, we know that once writers have a page to fix, they will tinker and polish dozens if not hundreds of times.

It is only once you've finished your first draft that you can truly enter the revision stage. Revisions are a vital part of the screenwriting process and we have some helpful advice for you about them.

REVISION PASSES

One of the benefits of The Talking Draft Method is that when you are able to quickly generate a first draft, you increase your chances of success by giving yourself more time to do revision work before your deadline. The work of revising and rewriting is where the actual work of a writer gets done.

The more times you can polish your script before sending it, the better you will progress professionally. A revision pass is a specific kind of careful and slow read-through of your finished draft with a red pen.

Here are some of the most fruitful and fun revision passes that writers use to polish their work. Each of these passes is one close read-through.

- Cut Adverbs – Remove words that end in "ly" because 99% of the time, any adverb you use can be improved upon and made into a more active and present-tense phrasing.

- Cut Gerunds – Passive voice will suck the energy out of your screenwriting if you allow it. Focus on what a person or thing does, not what is done to someone or something. Only use a verb that ends with "ing" when absolutely necessary.

- Cut Nows – Go through your story and search for the word "now" in an action line. Very often they are completely unnecessary.

- Cut Suddenlys – Search for the word "suddenly" in an action line. This word can nearly always be cut and the effect made more visceral by showing reaction to the suddenness.

- Cut "of the" from Action – Cutting this always improves your action.

- Cut Walks – Search your script for times that your action lines say that a character walks. Always change this word to a synonym with more personality: saunters, thunders, tiptoes, etc.

- Cut Sees – Search for word forms of the verb "to see" in your action lines. This can always be more evocative verb. Spies, glares, puzzles.

- Trim Justs – Do your characters say the word "just" too much? Active, forceful, assertive people (the types who drive the plot of a story) most likely do not flinch in their speech. Many meek or timid people say the word "just" as a way to couch any "ask" inside a cocoon of apologetic humility.

- Random polish – Jump to a random page and make it as effective as possible.

- Conflict Pass – Many scripts suffer from a syndrome where the conflict starts midway through a scene. Go through your script and edit the scenes so that the conflict starts closer to the top of the scene. When it comes to the shape of a scene, the adage is "start late and leave early."

- Subplot Pass – Go down the list of your supporting characters and imagine a famous actor in the role, now do a revision focusing solely on their experience of reading the script. The actor is hoping to see growth, a change, a glory beat, a moment for their acting reel. Not every subplot gets the obligatory "three scenes" that telegraph a growth from the beginning – through the middle – to a final beat. But it doesn't hurt.

- MC Pass – Scene-by-scene inspect who is driving the story. Is it your Main Character? If another character makes more decisions, takes more actions – or if the MC defers to others often, consider choosing a different protagonist or make your MC take the lead on more scene action. If after this reassessment, you don't know who your Main Character is, it is likely the person who changes the most over the course of the story.

- Story Pass – Do you have a situation or a story? Story needs a dilemma; a problem that can't be solved without creating another problem. Make sure that what your MC wants is impossible to achieve based on their current approach or identity.

- Backstory Pass – Make sure any details given about the backstory are absolutely critical to both character development and plot. If there is backstory mentioned that doesn't contain both character insight and plot details which are absolutely necessary, reevaluate whether this is absolutely relevant.

- The Spielberg Pass – In moments of awe, an audience surrogate character reacting on screen in tandem with the audience is helpful. Make sure that the audience sees how the characters feel about any incredible things they're seeing and experiencing. E.g. "Her jaw drops as…"

- The Sea Change Pass – Working backwards, look at where each of your characters ends up at the end of the story – note how they have changed emotionally. Then see how far from that place they can be at the beginning of the story. This will give them a greater character arc and it will give them room to grow.

- Choice Pass – Read through the script paying attention to one character's choices. A character is defined by two things: what she wants, and what she is willing to do to get it. This is revealed through the choices she makes. So for each character, make sure you give them a revealing choice when we meet them, and we will know who they are immediately. Repeat for each character.

- Power Pass – Go through the scenes with heavy dialogue remembering that dialogue is a debate about a choice. Whoever holds the choice holds the power. When possible, let the chooser be the one who overturns implicit character hierarchies. When possible, use a scene object to signify, visually, that choice.

- Anchor Pass – Because every paragraph of action is essentially a new camera setup, the first words in every action line become important indicators of camera placement. E.g. "High heels clomp" vs "She walks." These anchoring nouns position your reader's mind's eye in the right place without using the words "camera" or "we see."

- Logline in Header – Your logline is a one sentence description of the story. The sentence usually mentions the inciting incident, the protagonist, an action, and the antagonist. Put it in the header (or footer) of your document while revising to see a constant reminder of what you're aiming for.

- Icebox File – Keep a separate file for your project with the word "ICEBOX" in the file name to save your cuts. Every time you cut a scene or some dialog, paste it into your Icebox file. You never know when you'll need to reincorporate old cuts.

ON NOTES

Without fail, the more your story treatment or outline is bombarded with suggestions and questions from readers (i.e. what industry people call "notes"), the better your first draft will be.

As a professional, or a truly aspiring professional, there is no room or time for you to "discover" the story as you go. If and when you get the chance to pitch a movie idea, you have to tell them the ending. Buyers often have notes about the ending. They don't want to be surprised when they read your work – and they really don't want to find plot holes.

Fortunately you will have extra time to get your beat sheet and step-outline bulletproof. This is because there is no faster way to generate a first draft than with the Talking Draft Method.

Then, because your first draft can be done in a matter of days with the Talking Draft Method, you will also have extra time to polish and sit with your script as you revise before handing it in. The longer you have to rework your draft, the more opportunity you will have to address the kinds of notes that every script usually gets on the first rewrite.

Pre-address the standard notes before you send it to anyone. Assume these are the notes your first draft will get:

1.   the character conflict seems weak
2.   the story seems flat at times
3.   the plot seems hard to follow
4.   the dialogue sounds all the same / is too talky
5.   the scenes or characters seem repetitious
6.   could use more character development
7.   there's too much direction on the page
8.   the script didn't build to a satisfying end
9.   couldn't connect to the main character
10. the main character could use a love interest
11. the antagonist should be bad earlier

The more a writer sees these same obligatory notes, the better we get at answering them with added beats or extra details. Writer-Director Jordan Peele has this exact approach to his writing process – he thinks of it as a game. He assumes there will be dozens of drafts of every screenplay he writes. Writers contractually have to answer the scores of notes that bombard every script.

For Peele, the whole rewrite process game is a matter of decreasing the number of drafts it takes for him to get "no notes." Like in golf, where a perfect score is impossible, the game is to get your score as low as you can. Peele won't say how few drafts it takes to get him to "no notes" but rewriting is a game he takes seriously.

Jordan Peele's first drafts have already bent over backwards to satisfy the top eleven notes. If your first draft has ample evidence to satisfy the above list of common notes, you are way ahead of the game. The Talking Draft Method gives you the extra time to accomplish this.

"Sometimes you're swinging your way through a first draft like a blind miner with a pick-axe. That's okay. Just get it done."

- Screenwriter Justin Marks

The people giving you notes want you to hear their notes and hear the spirit of their notes. They want you to do something creative and original to address the heart of the note, without literally servicing all their idle musings and the things that they happen to just throw out in a notes meeting. So be creative when pre-addressing the standard notes.

Depending on the context provided by your reader's other notes, you may find that sometimes the obligatory note about a love interest could be serviced by enhancing the emotional stakes of the B-story. Maybe your main character just needs to show some additional emotion for *something*. Other times, your reader might actually be satisfied if you show your main character engaging in a hobby because what the reader was really reacting to was a certain flatness to your character's daily routine.

Answering notes is an important part of the job. Having the time to pre-address the most popular notes will get you better faster.

WHERE

FREED WRITING

Now that you know how and why to use The Talking Draft Method, you can create your stories everywhere.

The technology behind www.TalkingDraft.com is continually adding new languages to its speech-to-text engine. Therefore, the number of countries where writers can finally use the Talking Draft Method is always growing.

Where mobility is concerned, one technique that works very well with regard to achieving flow state creativity is to take the TalkingDraft.com website with you on a walk.

Many users report success when they use their computers to create a step-outline and program the speaking character names onto the application's 1-9 number buttons.

Then they close the webapp on their computer, open a web browser on their phone, plug in a microphone and take a walk while talking.

The number pad on your phone screen can be pressed with a finger or thumb and the app will work just as it does on your computer.

After your walk-and-talk, users close the browser on their phone, re-open the story on their computer's browser and export the file into their word processor.

Specifically where you walk is up to you. As long as there is Wi-Fi internet, or a cellular connection, you will be able to use www.TalkingDraft.com and channel the endorphins that come from kinetic activity into your walking Talking Draft.

Other users of the webapp use their computers and pace around their offices wearing a wireless headset and a Bluetooth keyboard's separate number pad numerical keyboard unit.

REASONS FOR TALKING

In summation, the major reasons to use the Talking Draft Method are these:

1.   Create Faster

A 20 minute dictation session leaves you with over 2000 words. Our goal is getting your first draft done fast. TalkingDraft.com gives you enough free speech-to-text transcription time for a feature film because we know you'll love it. With the Talking Draft Method, if you can picture the movie in your head, your first draft is as good as done!

2.   Convenience

TalkingDraft.com has invented the most screenwriter-friendly manual diarization process for creating scenes. Our speech-to-text technology is customized by-and-for screenwriters. Our text file output works with every major screenwriting application. Our story outliner guides writers to make a tight beat sheet using the latest popular movie structure styles.

3.   Calming Your Internal Editor

The problem with typing is that you get paralyzed with fear. You worry about crafting the perfect description. You fuss over using the correct grammar and punctuation. You are staring at a blank screen, in a quiet room, and nothing sparks your imagination. Talk it out instead. You can always press pause or spacebar if you need a second to think.

4.   Health Reasons

If you suffer from a repetitive stress injury, carpal tunnel, shaking hands, or experience numbness and pain in your fingers from typing, dictation is ideal. You can dictate standing up, or while walking around the room without having to type with your hands.

APPENDIX

For the following structure beat sheet models, if you want to see the suggested percentage of the story that each beat should occupy in your story, visit the free beat sheet calculator at www.ScriptOutliner.com. Although page number targets are helpful for novices and students, those target page numbers are merely suggestions.

The Eight Sequence System

In the 1970s and 80s, Frank Daniel taught his "8-Sequence" system at USC Film School and AFI. This divides your story into 8 sections of equal length, defined by various emotional and active characteristics. This system actually dates to when film projectors had to change the 15-minute-long reels of film stock. A two-hour movie needed 8 reels. Writers would end each sequence with a cliff-hanger to keep the audience from leaving. Thinking of each of these sequences as mini-movies can help you produce a film that has well-defined set-pieces like *Indiana Jones and the Last Crusade*.

1. Status Quo & Inciting Incident

Establishes the central character, their life, the status quo in the world of the story. Sequence one usually ends with the *Point of Attack* or *Inciting Incident*, but this plot point can sometimes appear earlier in the first few minutes of the film.

2. Predicament & Lock In

Sets up the *Predicament* that will be central to the story, with first glimpses of possible obstacles. The main tension is established at the end of the act. The sequence ends when the main character is *Locked In* the predicament, propelling her into a new direction to obtain her goal.

3. First Obstacle & Raising the Stakes

The *First Obstacle* to the central character is faced, and the beginning of the elimination of the alternatives begins, often a time where *Exposition* left over from Act 1 is brought out. Since our character is locked into the situation and can't simply walk away, there is a *Raising of The Stakes* with a lot more to lose.

4. First Culmination & Midpoint

A higher *Obstacle*, the principle of *Rising Action* is brought in and builds to the *First Culmination*, which usually parallels the *Resolution* of the film. If the story is a tragedy and our hero dies, then the first culmination (or midpoint) should be a low point for our character. If, however, our hero wins in the end of the film, then sequence four should end with her winning in some way.

5. Subplot & Rising Action

The second act sag may set in at this point if we don't have a strong *Subplot* to take the ball for a while. We still want *Rising Action*, but we're not ready for the *Main Culmination* yet.

6. Main Culmination & End of Act Two

The build-up to the *Main Culmination* - back to the main story line with vigor. The biggest obstacle, the last alternative, the highest or lowest moment and the end of our main tension come at this point. But we get the first inklings of the new tension that will carry us through the third act.

7. New Tension & Twist

The full yet simple, brief establishment of the third act tension with its requisite exposition. Simpler, faster in nearly all ways, with rapid, short scenes and no real elaborate set-ups. The *Twist* can end this sequence or come at the start of the eighth sequence.

8. Resolution

Hell-bent for the *Resolution*. Clarity is important. If they turn left, all is well, if they go right, the world as we know it ends. Not that we don't have complex emotions or ideas about what it all amounts to, but at this point we crave clarity. Will she get the girl, defuse the bomb, turn in her murderous brother and escape from the sinking boat?

Five-Act TV

Most hour-long network TV is built on a 5 Act structure adapted from classic playwright Gustav Freytag who wrote about how to craft well-formed stage plays. Some TV shows have a teaser and tag; these short scenes can be included in the first and fifth acts.

Act 1: Big start / Exposition

Introduce the main characters and backstory. Present the central dilemma through an "exciting force" or "inciting incident." Set off A and maybe B stories. Act ends with a "wow" moment that turns the story.

Act 2: Rising Action, Conflicts Appear

Things escalate. The conflict begins to increase as the characters try to achieve their goals. Expand the world, meet the characters of the C story. The different trajectories build your narrative toward the climax. C story has three scenes total.

Act 3: The Center, Things Get Real Bad, Climax

The third act contains the worst or most exciting beat, the moment where the tension reaches its peak. It features a turning point – not the culmination of action. At the midpoint, a change ushers in the "counterplay."

Act 4: Falling Action, Crush, Everything's Downhill

Story turns in a new direction, more evidence, or a big character revelation. A ticking clock triggers a series of events that build suspense and anxiety about how the story will unfold. Remember that the B story has at least one scene per act.

Act 5: Resolution / Tag

A moment of victory, the big reveal, ties up loose ends, brings the narrative to a close. Introduce a cliffhanger for the next episode.

The Hero's Journey

A narrative pattern identified by scholar Joseph Campbell dating from prehistory describes the typical Epic adventure of an archetypal "Hero." Christopher Vogler popularized Campbell's work when he was a story consultant for Walt Disney Pictures. These guideposts are not sections of equal length – some are individual moments within a longer sequence.

The Ordinary World

The hero, uncomfortable or unaware, is introduced sympathetically so the audience can identify with the dilemma. The hero is shown against a background of environment, heredity, and personal history. A polarity in the hero's life is pulling in different directions and causing stress.

The Call To Adventure

A moment when something shakes up the situation, either from external pressures or from something rising up from deep within, so the hero must face the beginnings of change.

Refusal Of The Call

The hero feels the fear of the unknown and tries to turn away from the adventure, however briefly. Alternately, another character may express the uncertainty and danger ahead.

Meeting With The Mentor

The hero comes across a seasoned traveler of the world who gives her training, equipment, or advice that will help on the journey. Or the hero reaches within to a source of courage and wisdom.

Crossing The Threshold

At the end of Act 1, hero leaves the Ordinary World and enters a new region or condition with unfamiliar rules and values: the Special World.

Tests, Allies and Enemies

The hero is tested and sorts out allegiances in the Special World.

Approach the Inner Cave

The hero and newfound allies prepare for the major challenge in the Special World.

The Ordeal

Near the middle of the story, the hero enters a central space in the Special World and confronts death or faces his or her greatest fear. Out of the moment of death comes a new life.

The Reward

The hero takes possession of the treasure won by facing death. There may be celebration, but there is also danger of losing the treasure again.

Chance to Make It Right

The hero heads back into the known world a changed person.

The Road Back

About three-fourths of the way through the story, the hero is driven to complete the adventure, leaving the Special World to be sure the treasure is brought home. Often a chase scene signals the urgency and danger of this mission.

The Resurrection

At the climax, the hero is tested once more on the threshold of home. He or she is purified by a last sacrifice, another moment of death and rebirth, but on a higher and more complete level. By the hero's action, the polarities that were in conflict at the beginning are finally resolved.

Return With The Elixir

The transformed hero returns home or continues the journey, bearing some element of the treasure that has the power to transform the world.

The Story Circle

TV scribe Dan Harmon teaches his writing staff to use his "Story Circle" system. This is a simplified version of the classic Hero's Journey framework that divides the story into eight sequences of equal length. This is especially good for stories that could be considered "there and back again" tales like *Mad Max: Fury Road* as well as standard sitcoms.

You

A character is in a zone of comfort.

Need

But they want something.

Go

They enter an unfamiliar situation.

Search

Adapt to it.

Find

Get what they wanted.

Take

Pay a heavy price for it.

Return

Then return to their familiar situation.

Change

Having changed.

The Six Stage Plot Structure

From Michael Hague, The Six Stage Plot Structure is a variation of the Three-Act plus the Hero's Journey. It is great for character-focused stories as it considers the inner journey as well as external goals. Over the course of six stages and five turning points, a character will stop living in fear and instead live courageously.

<u>ACT 1</u>

Inner journey stage 1: Character living fully within identity

We see the setting of Hero's everyday life. We establish identification with him, feel sympathy or anxiety for him, he's likeable or powerful.

Outer journey stage 1: The set-up

The physical circumstances of the story set-up (e.g. job, home).

Turning point 1: Opportunity

An event gives the character a decision and an external goal.

Inner journey stage 2: The character glimpses his destiny, it's a glimpse of living life in 'essence'

The hero should be presented with an opportunity that creates a desire. "Essence" is the spiritual, deeper self – who the hero really is.

Outer journey stage 2: New Situation

A first outward manifestation of the story and goal to aim for.

Turning point 2: Change of Plans

The hero is faced with a decision, a challenge that will transform his original desire into a visible goal with a specific end point. This is where the hero's outer motivation becomes clear and the story is in full swing.

<u>ACT 2</u>

Inner journey Stage 3: Moving towards Essence without leaving identity

As the character pursues her new goal, she gets scared, so she wavers between her identity and her essence.

Outer journey stage 3: Progress

Obstacles and conflict, but the hero seems to be managing these and overcoming them. Things seem to be working.

Turning Point 3: Point of No Return

The character must do something to show he's committed to the goal.

Inner journey Stage 4: Committed to essence but growing Fear

The hero struggles with difficult challenges but fears being her true self.

Outer journey stage 4: Complications and Higher Stakes

The conflict magnifies. The hero doesn't give up, he can't go back. Success feels within his grasp.

Turning Point 4: Major Setback

An 'all is lost' event occurs. The hero may attempt to hide behind his 'old life' mask again. Often a sidekick character will point out how he's stuck.

<u>ACT 3</u>

Inner journey Stage 5: Living one's Truth with everything to lose

The character returns to his essence; living true to his real self lets him 'earn' his success.

Outer journey stage 5: Final push

The hero has to face the outward manifestation of his quest, defeat the villain or find the prize.

Turning Point 5: Climax

The character must face his fear one final time to win the goal. The character's wound, weakness or fear should make another appearance here. The hero faces the biggest hurdle and the outer goal is resolved.

Inner journey Stage 6: The Journey complete, Destiny achieved

The character is now transformed and living in 'essence'. We get a glimpse of his new life.

Outer journey stage 6: Aftermath

The outer story is resolved, loose ends are tied up as the victory or defeat is now clear.

Pixar

The "Once upon a time…" story spine from Pixar.

Once upon a time…

In a few scenes introduce your character and setting. Your reader must know who this is about and where it is set to understand the story that is to follow.

And every day…

Explain to your reader what life is like in this world for your central character. Show this in a few scenes.

Until one day…

Something happens that forces change, what happens to set the story in motion? And the initial shockwaves.

And because of this…

Scenes that reveal what does your main character do, or want to achieve?

And because of that…

A first objective might be achieved, but what happens next? A new objective is good here. Short stories might skip this step.

Until finally…

This is the story's moment of truth, and then the final push or the big battle.

And ever since that day…

The close of the story tells us what this means for the central character.

The Debate

Screenwriter Drew Yanno came up with a format that builds your script into a teachable moment.

Question

Will the Protagonist get what is needed?

Debate

Ups and Downs are yes and no; differentiating what the character *needs* versus what they *want* is the crux of the inner journey.

Glimpse Answer

See the light at the end of the tunnel.

Setup Final Battle

Protagonist may set to answer the question of Act 1 or posit a new one.

The Final Battle

Is a Showdown.

Answers

Outcome of the battle answers the question from Act 1 or the new one.

Denouement

Reflection on the answer.

Bridge

A final explanation.

Life Torn Apart

Peter Dunne teaches his Life Torn Apart emotionally-centered structure.

Opening Scene

Establish the POV: the protagonist's emotional state and the story style.

State Problem

See the 1st Problem with supporting cast.

Meet Antagonist

The better the antagonist, the better the conflict; the better the conflict, the better the resolution; the better the resolution, the better the story.

Life As It Was

There is an apparent solution, a clash with co-protagonists, the solution disappears.

Problem Worsens

After the problem worsens, the choice is to take the easy way out or the hard way. We face a major crisis, the goals are set by the mentor, which results in a moral dilemma and/or doubt.

End of Act I

Life Will Never Be the Same

Danger Reveals Fear

Physical action creates risk and danger. Emotional resistance and fears are revealed

Co-Protagonist Feud

A feud causes doubt and distance

Emotional Turmoil

A case of fight or flight results in a loss. The route is altered.

Co-Protagonist Bonding

Fears are challenged and apartness is threatened in the bonding moment

The Middle

New danger defeats old weapons, our commitment to win, resulting in emotional defeat, loss of faith, hero is at her most vulnerable.

Co-Protagonist Commitment

An emotional union, changes begin, we see how growth is painful.

Co-Protagonist Offers Answers

And elicits acceptance, new reasons to stay and fight.

Deepest Fears are Tested

An emotional setback, here some might be willing to lose.

Higher purpose

Rebuild or die, alone again and sad, but the aloneness is no resolution.

New Set of Emotions

Facing death, the hero commit to love, faith defeats fears.

The Climax

Victory over the Antagonist, characters experience physical euphoria

Final Confrontation with Co-Protagonist

Emotional letdown, breakup with co-protagonist.

Mystery

The protagonist reflects on or faces the mysteries of life.

Victory over Fear

The resolution of the victory.

No Exit

Protagonist realizes you can't go home this way.

Let Go of Old Self

Letting go of old self, embracing co-protagonist, the emotional battle is finally won. Honestly facing feelings, causes trust and love.

Taking the Final Risk

For life as it is now.

Price Obtained

Happiness.

Seven Keys

David Trottier teaches that there tend to be seven key plot points in every well-developed story. He has written about this method for structuring screenplays.

Backstory

The Back Story haunts the central character.

Catalyst

The Catalyst gets the character moving. It's part of the story's setup.

Big Event

The Big Event changes the character's life.

Midpoint

The Midpoint is the point of no return or a moment of deep motivation.

Crisis

The Crisis is the low point, or an event that forces the key decision that leads to your story's end.

Showdown

The Showdown or Climax is the final face-off between your central character and the opposition.

Realization

The Realization occurs when your character and/or the audience sees that the character has changed or has realized something.

HartChart Guideposts

A-List Hollywood screenwriter James V. Hart teaches a popular method of diagnosing the health of your story's dynamics in accordance with the emotional highs and lows of the characters as they progress through the plot. In his masterclass for screenwriters, he introduces his terminology for the key beats that he tends to write towards.

Set the World

Let the audience meet your main characters and live in their world for a few minutes, size them up, empathize, worry, care a bit. This is what your main characters are doing the day before the movie starts.

New Opportunity

Your main character gets a new opportunity that could/will change the course of their life. What they do with that opportunity determines the course of the rest of your story.

2nd Opportunity

The second opportunity and what the main character does with the opportunity and the consequences of that opportunity puts the character in motion in pursuit of a new direction or new journey to achieve and obtain what the main character wants/needs.

Visible Tangible Goal

The choices your main character makes about the opportunities begins the journey of the story, and identifies a visible tangible goal your character(s) are trying to reach. This is also called the Desire Line: the line your main character follows in pursuit of his/her desire. This initial pursuit and identifying of the Visible Tangible goal usually occurs around the end of what many call Act 1.

Progress

Your main character makes progress toward the Visible Tangible Goal and deals with obstacles, characters, conflicts encountered that complicate the journey.

Setback

Something pushes your main character away from the Visible Tangible Goal. Progress and Setbacks are a series of mini-defeats and minor victories. Conflict and consequence comes with the decisions your main character makes that drive the story. There can be a number of short signposts for these.

Cinderella Moment

This gives to the main character a deserved moment of success in their struggle and empowers them to reach the *Top of the Mountain*. These moments typically occur more than once in your narrative.

Top of the Mountain

If you are drawing a picture of your movie, Top of the Mountain is typically near the center point of your narrative story. The highest point you have reached. Your main character has made progress toward their goal and realized a major/minor victory over some obstacle. Everything seems to be going according to plan. Your main character appears to be advancing toward their goal and what they want. There is a false sense of security as they reach a major summit. Now they must spend the rest of the story trying not to fall down the mountain.

Point of No Return

As your main character progresses to the Visible Tangible Goal, there comes a point where a decision, an action, or an event occurs, from which there is no turning back. It is too late to start over, what has happened cannot be undone or changed. The main character must continue toward the Visible Tangible Goal.

Plan Falls Apart

Your main character suffers a series of "apparent defeats" in order to achieve their goal. And just when it seems that all is going to work out, the Hero hits the wall. The rug is pulled out. The plan falls apart. Your Hero is down a hole or up that infamous creek with seemingly no way to reach their goal that their Desire Line has compelled them to seek.

The Resurrection

After your main character has crashed and burned and all is lost, you have a choice to make: do you leave your main character in flames on the desert floor, never to reach their goal or do you give them a resurrection opportunity, a chance to get back on their feet and complete their journey?

Conflict Resolution

Does your main character get what they want or not? Is it good or bad for them? Do they reach the Visible Tangible Goal? This section should address how your main character comes to grips with their nemesis. Their growth through the previous structure sign posts or lack of growth will determine whether or not they can successfully neutralize the nemesis and if they get what they want – or get what they need – or both.

Satisfying Ending

How do you want your audience to feel at the end and have you delivered a satisfying ending that has been earned and properly anticipated?

Giseungjeongyeol (기승전결)

Classic Chinese, Korean and Japanese narratives are based on a structure composed of four parts. Also called Kishōtenketsu, it is sometimes described as a narrative structure devoid of conflict.

Gi (기: rouse, wake up)

Raising issues and introducing characters. The reason a thing begins.

Seung (승: win, receive, be informed, earn)

The beginning of the action (but not to solve a problem, necessarily, but usually for self-realization). Processing hardships fills the majority of the story.

Jeon (전: and ever since, a turn)

A reversal or change in direction which crescendos near the center of this section close to the end.

Gyeol (결: incidental result)

The matter is concluded and any lessons are gained through the process or results are reflected upon.

ACKNOWLEDGEMENTS

This book would not be possible without my partner in all things Maggie Moon whose edits, support, suggestions, notes, and guidance on this book were invaluable. The screenwriting knowledge contained in this book came from my good fortune of knowing and learning from writing partners and mentors such as: James V. Hart, Bill Diamond, Jake Hart, Mal Young, Greg Pruss, Lance Gentile, Kevin Nicklaus, Ben Halm, Harold Pinter, and others whose friendship I cherish and whose privacy I respect. My connection to a fast first draft was honed in the workshops of Some Assembly Required LA, a brave theater and production ensemble which produced entire films and plays based on an audience suggestion in a matter of weeks. The "yes and" spirit of live theater that shaped me is thanks to those theater professionals I've had the great luck to work with including Lyndie Wright, Shannon Michael Wamser, Katie Locke O'Brien, Christopher Catalano, Travis Mitchell, Rich Fromm, Bryn Boice, Amy Herzog, Alex Timbers, Gregory Rae, Kyle Jarrow, Matthew O'Neill, Alan Cumming, Barnaby Harris, Eric Stoltz, and so many others. The writers and teachers who I have learned from are too many for this page but I must mention Christopher Vogler, David Trottier, Peter Dunne, Robert Towne, Drew Yanno, Andrew Stanton, Michael Hague, Dan Harmon, Frank Daniel, Blake Snyder, Corey Mandell, Alan Watt, and Jill Chamberlain. The automation of the Talking Draft Method at www.TalkingDraft.com would not have been possible without my technology partner Mark T. Sebastian who is one of those rare geniuses whose engineering mind is also that of an artist.